CONTENTS

Third printing 2010

TWENTY-THIRD PUBLICATIONS
A Division of Bayard
One Montauk Avenue, Suite 200
New London, CT 06320
(860) 437-3012 or (800) 321-0411
www.23rdpublications.com

The Scripture passages contained herein are from the *New Revised Standard Version of the Bible*, copyright ©1989, by the Division of Christian Education of the National Council of Churches in the U.S.A. All rights reserved.

ISBN 978-1-58595-735-4
Library of Congress Catalog Card Number: 2008943611

Printed in the U.S.A.

Published in Canada by Novalis
10 Lower Spadina Avenue, Suite 400
Toronto, Ontario, Canada
M5V 2Z2
www.novalis.ca

ISBN 978-2-89646-141-7

Cataloguing in Publication is available from Library and Archives Canada.

We acknowledge the financial support of the Government of Canada through the Book Publishing Industry Development Program (BPIDP) for our publishing activities.

EXPERIENCE
Walking the Sacred Path
Concert and Lenten Retreat...

A reflective weekend of song and retreat for all who are seeking
a deeper relationship with God as we begin the Holy Week.

FEATURING: DAN SCHUTTE

Dan has been composing music for worship for more than 30
years, including extensive collaboration with the St. Louis Jesuits. His
more recent pieces exhibit an enduring ability to reach into people's
hearts and draw them into prayer. He is one of the best-known, most
prolific and influential composers of music for the liturgy today.

HOSTED BY: INCARNATION–ST. JAMES CATHOLIC CHURCH

1545 Pennington Road. | Ewing, NJ 08618

An Evening with Dan Schutte (Parish Concert)
Friday, March 30, 2012 – 7 PM

Walking the Sacred Path (Parish Retreat/Workshop)
Saturday, March 31, 2012: 10 AM – 1 PM
Lunch will be served

Here I Am, Lord (Parish Reflection)
Saturday, March 31, 2012 – Following the 5:30 PM Mass

Let Us Go to the Altar (Parish Reflection)
Sunday, April 1, 2012: – Following the 5:30 PM Mass

Finding Your Sacred Path:
A Journey in Song and Story

Friday Evening,
March 30, 2012
Parish Concert with
Composer Dan Schutte

Walking the
sacred
path

Dan Schutte

Take Comfort in the Lord, Our God

Saturday, March 31, 2012
10:00 AM—1:30PM
Parish Retreat & Workshop
"Walking the Sacred Path, A Lenten Retreat."

Saturday, March 31, 2012
Following the 5:30PM Mass at Incarnation
Parish Reflection Talk
"Here I am Lord." & Adoration

Sunday, April 1, 2012
Following the 5:30 PM Mass at Incarnation
Parish Reflection Talk
"Let Us Go to the Altar" & Adoration

Incarnation-St. James Parish
1545 Pennington Road, Ewing, NJ 08618

A Lenten Retreat
With Composer Dan Schutte

Sponsored by Incarnation-St. James
Church

March 30-April 1, 2012

Introduction

A group of business professionals was gathered for their monthly luncheon. As was their custom once each year, they invited their pastors to join them. After the meal they had scheduled a famous actor to provide some entertainment as people were enjoying coffee and dessert. The actor stood before them dramatically reciting lines from famous plays and poetry. At one point he invited requests from those in attendance. One elderly priest rose and spoke. "Would you recite for us Psalm 23?" The actor, a bit surprised by the unusual request, finally agreed. "Father," he said," I'll agree to your request under one condition. After I recite the psalm, I'd be honored if you would then recite it too." Reluctantly, the elderly priest agreed.

So the actor presented a stunningly beautiful recitation of Psalm 23, to which people responded with enthusiastic applause. Then he turned to the priest and said, "Okay, Father, your turn." So the priest rather hesitantly stood and began reciting the famous psalm. "The Lord is my shepherd. There is nothing I shall want."

When he finished, there was no applause, just hushed silence. The people, so moved by his simple recitation, were sitting with tears running down their faces. After a few moments the actor rose and spoke. "Ladies and gentlemen, I spoke to your ears. But this man has spoken to your hearts. And here's the difference. I know Psalm 23. But this man knows the Shepherd."

Sometimes we mistakenly think that our faith is about understanding the truths of our faith, or professing a particular creed of

1

beliefs, or learning the Holy Scriptures. But these things are only secondary. Our faith, at its core, is about our relationship with God, and with Jesus, the one who showed us the face of God.

St. Ignatius of Loyola, best known for his handbook for retreats, truly understood this. The *Spiritual Exercises* are essentially a journey with Jesus. Through a series of "contemplations," a retreatant follows Jesus through his life, from his birth to resurrection. By watching Jesus, listening, spending time with him, a person is drawn into a deeper relationship with him. Jesus becomes both our Lord and friend, and we become his disciples. This is the heart of our faith.

The "exercises" in this book are loosely based on the *Spiritual Exercises* of St. Ignatius. Their goal is the same: to draw a person into a real, living, growing relationship with Jesus. But the language is simple and prayerful and certainly not intimidating for anyone wishing to pray this way. And these exercises are based on the same concept of contemplation as the means to achieve a deeper relationship with Jesus.

The prayer of contemplation may be a bit new to some. It should not be confused with meditation, which can be primarily an intellectual venture of coming to "understand" the meaning of a Scripture passage. Contemplation certainly involves understanding, but it embraces an understanding of both the heart and mind. In contemplative prayer a person uses the power of imagination to enter into the story of Jesus as presented in Scripture. We allow ourselves to become one of the people in the Bible story, to see, hear, smell, taste, and respond to what is going on.

These exercises are not just for special times of retreat. You can use them just as effectively in your daily prayer. But they do require a commitment of time. This kind of prayer cannot be rushed. Do them when you can set aside a half hour or more to spend time with God. You might imagine it as time you are spending in the presence of your dearest friend. This is not a prayer of words. In fact, it is better to imagine ourselves as simply watching and listening than to feel compelled to say something. This may be hard for many of us and may take some time to get used to. But it is well worth the effort.

Each of the following exercises provides four elements designed to be of help during the time of prayer: 1) Preparation, 2) Reflection, 3) Things to Consider, and 4) Closing Prayer. These are meant to provide a place to begin and a bit of structure. However, the most important thing when we pray is that we follow the lead of God's Spirit. As we enter into the prayer, we may find ourselves drawn in another direction. Or we may find that one particular point, or one image, seems to capture our heart and our attention. These are moments of grace and we should always stay in that place and savor the goodness of them. Please don't feel compelled to rush to finish the entire exercise. Rather, stay with what brings you light, freedom, peace, and consolation.

As you work your way through these contemplations, it's very helpful to keep a prayer journal or notebook to write down your reflections and experiences. This is a wonderful way to remember what happened as you prayed. Sometimes there may not be much to write because the journey of prayer also includes moments of emptiness and barrenness when it seems that nothing is happening. But at other times there will be moments of great consolation and intimacy with Jesus. A prayer journal can help you hold onto these and allow you to look back and see more clearly the hand of God in your life.

St. Ignatius's notion of a person in relationship with Jesus is that he or she becomes a "contemplative in action." By this he meant that prayer would become such a part of our lives that the line separating times of prayer and the rest of our daily activity would begin to fade. In other words, we can begin to carry our prayerfulness with us as we go about our daily activities. When we love someone, we carry the presence of that person with us even when we're not consciously thinking about them. Those we love may come to mind for a few moments while we are driving in the car or doing our grocery shopping. And we spend a few moments being grateful for their presence in our lives. This same dynamic can be true of our relationship with God.

Some people find that music helps them to pray. Each exercise will suggest an appropriate piece of music to accompany it. (An Appendix in the back of the book lists the collections where you can find each of these pieces of music.) You might use the piece of music to help quiet your soul and focus your mind and heart. Or you might play the music throughout your day to help you recall your time of prayer. If the music is helpful, use it. If not, it's certainly not necessary to the integrity of these exercises.

As Christians we are commissioned by the Risen Jesus to be witnesses of what we have seen and heard:

> *Now the eleven disciples went to Galilee, to the mountain to which Jesus had directed them. When they saw him, they worshiped him; but some doubted. And Jesus came and said to them, "All authority in heaven and on earth has been given to me. Go therefore and make disciples of all nations, baptizing them in the name of the Father and of the Son and of the Holy Spirit, and teaching them to obey everything that I have commanded you. And remember, I am with you always, to the end of the age."*
>
> ❧ MATTHEW 28:16–20

The Good News that we proclaim and witness to is not something written in a book. It is a Person. May these contemplation exercises help you to come to know and love Jesus in a new way. Walk with him on the sacred path and he will reveal himself to you. And most of all, you will come to know how much he loves you.

So great our hunger

SUGGESTED MUSIC
"Beyond the Moon and Stars"

PREPARATION
Find a quiet place where you will not be disturbed or distracted. Take a comfortable, relaxed sitting position. Recall that prayer is more about listening than speaking, so do not worry about what words to speak. Prepare yourself by closing your eyes and focusing on your breathing. Spend a couple of minutes sitting quietly, inhaling and exhaling deep, long breaths. There's no need to rush. Slowly become mindful of God's loving presence, both around you and within you. Sit and take in the comfort and peace that the Lord's presence brings. When you're ready, continue by prayerfully reading the following reflection.

REFLECTION
> *O God, you are my God,*
> *I seek you,*
> *My soul thirsts for you;*
> *My flesh faints for you,*
> *as in a dry and weary land*
> *where there is no water.*
> 🖝 PSALM 63

Hunger motivates us. In both the physical and spiritual realms, our energies are often focused on satisfying our hunger. St. Ignatius of Loyola understood this. In his handbook for spiritual growth, the *Spiritual Exercises*, he invites us to reflect prayerfully on our deepest desires. What do I most want in life? What excites me? What are my hopes and dreams? In his wisdom, Ignatius knew that getting in touch with our deepest desires and longings is the key to finding where God is working in our lives.

In our living we do experience moments of deep and profound happiness. But we also realize that the satisfaction they bring is only temporary. Before we know it, we've moved on to the next dream, ever hoping that the next horizon will make us happy. We hunger for love, for intimacy, for belonging, for accomplishment, for peace, for justice, for the happiness of our children, for our first home, for a life companion, for health, for wealth, and for security. And even though we experience the joy that these bring, we still hunger for something more.

No one likes being hungry. In our hurry, we often look for satisfaction in things that ultimately are not good for us, and maybe even hurt us or the ones we love. Sometimes we turn to unhealthy relationships, addictive chemicals, food, sex, alcohol, or work because we are frantic to do something about this ache that exists at the core of our being. We hate it. It's not a comfortable feeling, and so we often try to run from it. Instead, at the beginning of his *Spiritual Exercises*, St. Ignatius suggests that we need to spend time with our hunger. Rather than running from it and trying not to feel it, we are invited to stay with our hunger and learn from it.

Where does this deep down, soulful hunger come from? The ache that you and I experience deep in our souls was created by the One in whose image we are made. We are meant for God and God is meant for us. While we look for many ways to satisfy the hunger of our hearts, ultimately we will only find satisfaction in the heart of God.

If we really believe that we are created in the image and likeness of God, it makes sense that the same hunger that is so much a part of us is somehow a part of God's being as well. Our insatiable thirst for happiness and intimacy was created by a God who longs to be in union with us. The entire story of salvation is about the unreserved love of God that constantly draws us into the intimacy and companionship for which we were created.

> *Three times I appealed to the Lord about this, that it would leave me, but he said to me, "My grace is sufficient for you, for power is made perfect in weakness." So, I will boast all the more gladly of my weaknesses, so that the power of Christ may dwell with me.*
>
> *Therefore I am content with weaknesses, insults, hardships, persecutions, and calamities, for the sake of Christ; for whenever I am weak, then I am strong.*
>
> 🖎 2 CORINTHIANS 12:8–11

Perhaps the most precious thing we can offer each other on this journey of faith is a willingness to let others know the hunger of our own hearts. This means that we must find the courage to be vulnerable to each other. This is never an easy thing. But by offering others a glimpse into our own journey of faith, we give them hope and let them know they are not alone. When we speak from our weakness, without the arrogance of thinking we have all the answers, we offer the greatest gift.

THINGS TO CONSIDER

Take some time to pray about the following questions:

- In the depths of my soul, what do I most desire?
- What are my greatest hopes and dreams?
- How do I try to satisfy the longings of my soul? Where do I seek happiness?
- What do I seek that really doesn't satisfy my hunger?
- During this time of reflection, what most moves my soul?

If you have a prayer journal, write down your answers so that you can remember them and come back to them later.

CLOSING PRAYER

Ignatius ends each of his exercises with a "colloquy," a heartfelt prayer, in one's own words, addressed to the God who loves us and is present here with us. It should be spoken like a friend talking to a friend. You may begin with the following words, and then continue to talk to God however your heart moves you.

Ever faithful God,
open the windows of my heart
to allow your peace to enter those places
where I most need refreshment.
Help me, O Lord,
to recognize the hunger you created in me,
to be aware of the deepest desires of my heart,
to know that I will find you in my longing.
Deepen my faith, dear God,
that I might walk in faith beside you
in companionship with those you've given me to
*   love.*

The story of God in my life

SUGGESTED MUSIC
"Dayenu Litany"

PREPARATION
Find a quiet place where you will not be disturbed or distracted. Take a comfortable, relaxed sitting position. Prepare yourself by closing your eyes and focusing on your breathing. Spend a couple of minutes sitting quietly, inhaling and exhaling deep, long breaths. Slowly become mindful of God's loving presence, both around you and within you. When you're ready, continue by prayerfully reading the following reflection.

REFLECTION
> *For I am convinced that neither death nor life,*
> *nor angels, nor rulers,*
> *nor things present, nor things to come,*
> *nor powers, nor height, nor depth,*
> *nor anything else in all creation,*
> *will be able to separate us from the love of God*
> *in Christ Jesus our Lord.*
> > ❧ ROMANS 8:38–39

9

God is abundantly generous with us. We don't often take the time to reflect on all the ways God has blessed our lives, but that's the purpose of this exercise. We're going to pay special attention to God's bounty to us as we explore significant memories.

As you do this exercise, imagine God sitting beside you. Together you're going to go through a photo album of your life. In this album are many memories—people, events, successes, failures, happiness, tragedy, and pain. These snapshots capture special memories in the story of your life and all of them together bring you to this day and this moment.

Each photograph from our memory album has a feeling attached to it. Sometimes the memories are happy ones, easy to stay with and embrace with peace. But sometimes the feelings these snapshots evoke will be painful, embarrassing, sad, or fearful. When you experience these difficult feelings, remember that God is there at your side. How did God guide you during these difficult moments of your life? Sometimes in looking back we will be able to recognize how God brought us to a new and better place.

We're not trying to search out long-forgotten or hidden memories, but perhaps you'll remember something that you haven't thought of in a long time. Take this as a sign that God may want you to discover something new and important in it. But most of the memories will be familiar ones because they are part of your often-told story. Whether the memory is familiar or foreign, look for God's guiding hand.

Our photo albums are really not as much about us as they are about how much God loves us. True love yearns to reveal itself. If we take the time and look with the eyes of faith, each of the photos in our album is an example of God revealing love and care for us. God wants to tell us over and over again how much we are loved. Love expresses itself more perfectly in deeds than in words. The grace of this exercise is to allow ourselves to be overwhelmed by this love.

God is in love with us, and like a good lover, God courts us and woos us with signs and symbols of love. When we don't get it, God tries again and again, all the while hoping that we will finally take notice. Each of the photos is a symbol of God's faithful care and steadfast love. God won't give up until we finally get the message. When we finally allow God to love us, the power of that love is transforming.

Now take some time to look at the photos of the middle of your life. Allow yourself to experience the feelings attached to these. Let God show you how he was present in these memories. When you're finished, write down some of the important ones.

And finally, look over the photos of your recent life's story. These will be the fresh memories, but surely filled with feeling. Which of the photos are most important? Which make you smile? Or weep? Or laugh?

God sees us just as we are, and yet loves us beyond words. God's love does not depend on our holiness or perfection. Even beyond that, there is nothing we can do to earn God's love. It is simply a freely given, gracious gift. And what if we could see ourselves as God sees us? What possibly could keep God from loving us? The truly amazing thing is that there is nothing at all, not even sin, that can keep God from loving us.

THINGS TO CONSIDER

Take some time to pray about the following questions:

- As you look at the photos of your life, how do you feel about them?
- What are the happiest? The saddest?
- How did they influence who you are today?
- How was God present in each of them?
- Do you think God sees them the same way that you do?

If you have a prayer journal, write down your answers so that you can remember them and come back to them later.

CLOSING PRAYER

Using one's imagination to pray is not pretending. St. Ignatius in his *Spiritual Exercises* often invites a person to use a form of imaginative prayer. It's a powerful way to use the mind and heart to connect with God.

For a few minutes close your eyes and imagine God's face before you. Let yourself see the features of his face. Look into his eyes. Let him look into your eyes. And finally, imagine God smiling as he looks at you. He is proud and takes great delight in you, his beloved one. Don't rush to move on. Let yourself bask in the loving gaze of God.

When you are finished, end with the following prayer or with a prayer in your own words.

Dear God, Lord of my life,
I sit in awe before the gaze of your love.
It is sometimes difficult to let you love me in this
   way.
I'm not used to its power and warmth.
But I want to let your love transform me
so that I can become a better disciple,
a better companion of your Son Jesus.
Set me ablaze with the fire of that love.

Teach me to be generous

SUGGESTED MUSIC
"Christ Circle Round Us"

PREPARATION
Find a quiet place where you will not be disturbed or distracted. Take a comfortable, relaxed sitting position. Recall that prayer is more about listening than speaking, so do not worry about what words to speak. Prepare yourself by closing your eyes and focusing on your breathing. Spend a couple of minutes sitting quietly, inhaling and exhaling deep, long breaths. There's no need to rush. Slowly become mindful of God's loving presence, both around you and within you. Sit and take in the comfort and peace that the Lord's presence brings. When you're ready, continue by prayerfully reading the following reflection.

REFLECTION
"Now when they first came, they thought they would receive more; but each of them also received the usual daily wage. When they received it, they grumbled against the landowner, saying, 'These last worked only one hour, and you have made them equal to us who have borne the burden of the day and the scorching heat.' But he replied to one of them, 'Friend, I am doing you no

13

wrong; did you not agree with me for the usual daily wage?...I
choose to give to this last the same as I give to you.'"

MATTHEW 20:10–14

Our God is amazingly generous and wants to give us everything
with no limits. In fact, God desires our happiness more than we do.
God wants us to know the kind of joy that comes only through intimacy. God wants us to grow in holiness and love. There's just one
hitch. We've been given the gift of freedom and so we can refuse
God. We can close our hearts to the work God desires to do in us.
We can block the way to our becoming holy men and women.

At the beginning of his *Spiritual Exercises*, St. Ignatius encourages
a person to pray for a generous heart. He understands how important it is to be receptive to God's grace. If we open ourselves, there is
no end to the wonders God can and will do in us. God wants us to
become holy men and women, and to become bearers of the Good
News to others. God desires that we grow in faith so that we might
become more effective catechists and teachers.

Growing in holiness is not our doing, but rather, God's work in
us. People do not become saints because of how hard they have
tried to be good, but because they have allowed God to take over
their lives. We are God's work of art, and God is laboring in our
souls to slowly but surely create something amazingly beautiful.
When we are generous with God, he can mold us and fashion us
into his holy people. Most of our job is just to stay out of the way
and not put up walls that keep God out.

When we explore the Old and New Testament Scriptures, it
becomes clear that the Holy One of Israel is very generous. First,
there's the bounty of creation. Then there's the generous promise
of the covenant with the people of Israel. Again and again God
shows mercy on his people who repeatedly turn away from him
and grumble when things aren't going right. God sends one prophet after another to speak to the people, to encourage them, to chide
them, to remind them of God's care. And finally, God sends his
own son, Jesus, to reveal the depth of his love.

God doesn't have to do any of this. There's nothing on our part that warrants such goodness and generosity. So why would God go so out of the way to shower us with kindness? Sometimes we get confused and think that we can somehow earn God's kindness. The Hebrew people thought that if they scrupulously kept the commandments and carefully followed the prescribed religious practices, then God would take care of them and bless them with bounty. They believed God's love was dependent upon their goodness. They thought they could somehow win God's favor.

In his teaching, Jesus of Nazareth is very clear that God's love is a free gift. There is nothing we can do to earn God's favor. Living a holy, good life and doing good deeds does not make God love us more. Rather, living a holy, faithful life is our response to God's overflowing generosity, not a means of earning God's love.

Everything we have is a gift, starting from the basic fact that we've been given the gift of life. But envy can cause us to question the wisdom of God in dispensing his bounty as he sees fit. We are sometimes arrogant enough to think that we'd know better how God's gifts should be distributed.

THINGS TO CONSIDER

Take some time to pray about the following questions:

- Do I want God in my life? Can I allow God to change me?
- Am I afraid of that? What are some of the ways I resist God?
- How does envy show itself in my life?
- Am I angry with God because I think I deserve more than I get?
- Are there ways in which I try to earn God's love?

If you have a prayer journal, write down your answers so that you can remember them and come back to them later.

CLOSING PRAYER

End your time of prayer by asking God for the grace you desire, from God, in this case the grace of generosity of mind and heart so that we might be able to receive God's bounty. Begin with the words that follow, and then continue to talk to God in your own words.

Thank you, dear Lord,
for your overwhelming generosity.
You have been so good to me.
I want you in my life, my lord.
Circle round me. Enfold me.
Break down my resistance to your love,
and heal the envy of my heart.
Give me a generous spirit and in everything
help me to trust your love for me.

The beauty of God

SUGGESTED MUSIC
"For the Beauty"

PREPARATION
Find a quiet place where you will not be disturbed or distracted. Take a comfortable, relaxed sitting position. Recall that prayer is more about listening than speaking, so do not worry about what words to speak. Prepare yourself by closing your eyes and focusing on your breathing. Spend a couple of minutes sitting quietly, inhaling and exhaling deep, long breaths. There's no need to rush. Slowly become mindful of God's loving presence, both around you and within you. Sit and take in the comfort and peace that the Lord's presence brings. When you're ready, continue by prayerfully reading the following reflection.

REFLECTION
Long ago God spoke to our ancestors
in many and various ways by the prophets,
but in these last days he has spoken to us by a Son,
whom he appointed heir of all things….
He is the reflection of God's glory
and the exact imprint of God's very being.
       ❧ HEBREWS 1:1–3

Some have said that the experience of beauty is the forgotten key to open the soul to God. We will often focus our efforts on disseminating those truths of doctrine and those teachings of Christ that are central to our faith. While these may be important, they don't usually lead us to an experience of God. God remains at most a fascinating idea or a reasonable truth. We can talk forever about God, but until we experience the presence of God, we do not really "know" the Lord.

Beauty is like a window into the divine. Just as the soul of any artist is revealed in the art they create, so too the soul of God, the Great Artist, is revealed in the world that is the work of God's hands. If we take the time to see the beauty of this world with new eyes, we will be drawn into the heart of the Holy One.

Treasures of great beauty surround us, sometimes forgotten or overlooked as we hurry about our lives. They can be found in physical beauty, the vitality of youth and the wisdom of age, the mysteries of science, in acts of justice and forgiveness, moments of love and intimacy, and even in intense grief. Beauty is not always pretty. While it can be seen in the harmonious lines of a Michelangelo sculpture, it can also be found in the deep furrowed wrinkles of an old woman.

Hans Urs von Balthasar, one of the great Catholic theologians of the twentieth century, believed that the real starting point for human encounter with God is an aesthetic experience of beauty, a brief glimpse of the glory of God manifest in nature or in a work of art. This experience takes us beyond ourselves, and into the realm of mystery and transcendence. Balthasar urges us to read Scripture from a new perspective. He suggests that the word "glory," as used in the Old and New Testaments, is synonymous with "beauty."

The heavens are telling the [beauty] of God;
and the firmament proclaims his handiwork.
   ❦ PSALM 19:1

Every valley shall be lifted up,
and every mountain and hill be made low....

Then the [beauty] of the Lord shall be revealed,
and all people shall see it together.
🌢 ISAIAH 40:4–5

Beauty has the power to transform the soul and instill gratitude as other things cannot. In truth, the experience of true beauty leads us to adoration, to worship. Pierre Teilhard de Chardin, the great Jesuit anthropologist and mystic, offers his own poetic voice in describing how beauty leads us to worship:

All around us, to right and left, in front and behind, above and below, we have only to go a little beyond the frontier of sensible appearances in order to see the divine welling up and showing through. But it is not only close to us, in front of us, that the divine presence has revealed itself. It has sprung up universally, and we find ourselves so surrounded and transfixed by it, that there is no room left to fall down and adore it, even within ourselves.

By means of all created things, without exception, the divine assails us, penetrates us, and molds us. We imagined it as distant and inaccessible, whereas in fact we live steeped in its burning layers….The world, this palpable world, which we were wont to treat with the boredom and disrespect with which we habitually regard places with no sacred association for us, is in truth a holy place, and we did not know it.
🌢 PIERRE DE TEILHARD DE CHARDIN,
THE DIVINE MILIEU

THINGS TO CONSIDER
Take a moment now to pray about the following questions.
- How and where do I experience beauty?
- Do I allow beauty to be a part of my life?
- How can I bring more beauty into my daily life?
- How can I make the experience of beauty a part of my prayer?

If you have a prayer journal, write down your answers so that you can remember them and come back to them later.

CLOSING PRAYER

Close your eyes and for a few moments picture something beautiful that you saw today. Stay with that image and take its goodness into your soul. You don't need to say anything. Just allow your heart to be moved to adoration of the Creator of such breathtaking majesty.

When you're ready, continue with the following prayer, or with a prayer in your own words. Speak to God as the child of God that you are, with your heart fully open to him.

Great and wonderful God,
I stand here in awe
before this beauty you have created.
It is just one reflection of the goodness that is yours.
I ask for the grace to open my soul to the beauty that
*   surrounds me,*
often hiding beneath the surface of things,
sometimes missed because I am moving so fast.
There is so much brutality and ugliness in this world
and I need to be reminded
that there is abundant goodness
and extraordinary beauty here too.

Found by love

SUGGESTED MUSIC
"So the Love of God"

PREPARATION
Find a quiet place where you will not be disturbed or distracted. Prepare yourself by closing your eyes and focusing on your breathing. Slowly become mindful of God's loving presence, both around you and within you. Then ask God for the grace of this exercise, which is to see in a new way the shame of sin and the horror of evil in this world. When you're ready, continue by prayerfully reading the following reflection.

REFLECTION
But God proves his love for us in that while we were still sinners Christ died for us. Much more surely then, now that we have been justified by his blood, will we be saved through him from the wrath of God. For if while we were enemies, we were reconciled to God through the death of his Son, much more surely, having been reconciled, will we be saved by his life. But more than that, we even boast in God through our Lord Jesus Christ, through whom we have now received reconciliation.

❧ ROMANS 5:8–10

Sin is not pretty and true evil is horrific. The reality of our world is that sin and evil exist right alongside breathtaking goodness and beauty. But we would much rather ignore the sin in our lives and anesthetize ourselves to the evil that surrounds us. It is not easy to look evil squarely in the eye, to see it for exactly what it is. But we do this with God's strong, reassuring hand on our shoulder, ever reminding us of the power of saving mercy.

This whole world—every animal and human being, the wind and sea, the moon and stars—was created good and beautiful by God. Sin enters this world when we twist and distort that goodness and beauty into something it was never meant to be. For example, the wonders of scientific knowledge can be used to save lives or destroy thousands. Terrible things are done every day in the name of love.

Evil is not just an abstract concept used to describe bad things and bad people. It is a living reality, a power moving in this world and in our lives. We might refer to this power as Satan or, as St. Ignatius—ever the soldier—named it: the "Enemy." Naming evil is important to Ignatius because there is nothing the Enemy wants more than for us to ignore him or to think he doesn't exist. The Enemy we name can no longer have power over us.

Unfortunately, evil doesn't exist just in newspapers, on television, or the Internet; it dwells within each of us. We ourselves contribute to the distortion of beauty and goodness, often showing our own irreverence for the gifts of God. And over time, our sin becomes a pattern in our life, so habitual that we become blind to its destructiveness.

But in the face of great evil, God's mercy is infinite. The shameful death of Jesus on a cross proves that God will spare nothing when it comes to our salvation, even the life of his own beloved Son. But what if we don't want to be saved? John Kavanaugh, SJ, professor of philosophy, author, and homilist, writes about our human reaction to God's mercy in his *Faces of Poverty* (Orbis Books).

> *"No, I am not worth your death. I was not worth your life and love. I am not worth your efforts, your forgiveness, your suffer-*

ing, your passion." This is the response we give when we are so overcome by our own sin that we think it is greater than God's creation, more lasting that God's love, and more compelling than God's beauty."

Or even more tragic:

"Thanks, but no thanks. You see, I do not need your love. I do not need your suffering and your bleeding heart. I do not want your forgiveness and your redeeming labors. For I am a 'self-made' person. I did it on my own. I pulled myself up by my own boot-straps. The others may need your death, your love, but not me."

We look to Jesus to see how a child of God responds to evil. He does not lash out. He does not repay evil by creating more evil. Rather, Jesus takes the evil into himself, suffers the horror and sadness, and redeems our sin with his love. Whenever we experience sin and evil, even our own, our best companion is Jesus the Risen One who shows us the wounds in his hands and feet, the marks of evil that have been transformed by God's most amazing love.

THINGS TO CONSIDER

Take a moment now to read today's news from the newspaper or on the Internet.

- Let your heart feel the day's events as fully as possible. Picture what the day would be like if love prevailed.
- In the presence of Christ on the cross, look at the sin of your life. How are you vulnerable to the tempting of the Evil Spirit?
- Can you let God love you? Do you think you're worthy of God's love?
- How can you allow God's saving love to change your heart and how you live?

If you have a prayer journal, write down your answers so that you can remember them and come back to them later.

CLOSING PRAYER

Close your eyes and for a few moments imagine yourself in the presence of Jesus, the Crucified Risen Lord. Let him show you the marks of his wounds. Speak to him about what's on your mind and in your heart in the following words, or better yet, in your own words.

Dearest Savior,
I stand in horror at the evil I see in this world
and want to run from it or simply ignore it.
Even more, I want to run from the evil
  in my own life.
I don't understand how you can still love me,
  and yet I know you do.
I see how you have embraced my sin, taken it upon
  yourself,
and redeemed it with a love
that is beyond what I can fathom.
Please help me to allow the power of your love to
  transform me.

Nothing is impossible for God

SUGGESTED MUSIC
"Come, O Lord"

PREPARATION

In this exercise we begin to use a kind of prayer that St. Ignatius in his *Spiritual Exercises* calls "contemplation." Using the power of imagination, we enter a Scripture passage, not only to understand it, but beyond that, to actually experience it in our own hearts. This kind of prayer takes the story beyond its surface details and allows it to come alive for us.

Don't worry if the prayer of contemplation feels awkward at first. It may take some practice before it begins to feel natural and comfortable. If you feel self-conscious at first, that's normal. Stay with it. Focus on opening your heart and imagination and they will reveal new depths of Scripture to you. It will also change your relationship with God.

As usual, find a quiet place and put yourself in the loving presence of God. Then begin by asking God for the grace you desire. In this exercise it will be to trust God's love enough to surrender your life into his hands.

REFLECTION

Read the following Scripture text slowly through once.

In the sixth month the angel Gabriel was sent by God to a town in Galilee called Nazareth, to a virgin engaged to a man whose name was Joseph, of the house of David. The virgin's name was Mary. And he came to her and said, "Greetings, favored one! The Lord is with you." But she was much perplexed by his words and pondered what sort of greeting this might be.

The angel said to her, "Do not be afraid, Mary, for you have found favor with God. And now, you will conceive in your womb and bear a son, and you will name him Jesus. He will be great, and will be called the Son of the Most High, and the Lord God will give to him the throne of his ancestor David. He will reign over the house of Jacob forever, and of his kingdom there will be no end."

Mary said to the angel, "How can this be, since I am a virgin?" The angel said to her, "The Holy Spirit will come upon you, and the power of the Most High will overshadow you; therefore the child to be born will be holy; he will be called the Son of God. And now, your relative Elizabeth in her old age has also conceived a son; and this is the sixth month for her who was said to be barren. For nothing will be impossible with God." Then Mary said, "Here am I, the servant of the Lord; let it be with me according to your word." Then the angel departed from her.

❧ LUKE 1:26–38

Put down the text, perhaps close your eyes, and use your imagination to picture the scene with as much detail as you can. Where is it taking place? Look around to see what things look like. What sounds do you hear? What do you smell? Who is there? Picture the young Mary of Nazareth. What do her clothes look like? Notice the expression on her face. What is she doing? How does the angel Gabriel come to her? What does he look like? Listen to their voices.

Place yourself in the scene, either as one of the principal characters or simply as a bystander.

Now go back and read the text again, pausing after each line. Begin to hear what's being said and watch the faces as the events unfold. Let the story proceed however your imagination takes you. The details of the text will cease to be important. If a particular moment seems significant, stay with it and savor it. Most of all let your heart feel what's going on. Take your time. There's no need to move forward until you're ready.

Nothing is impossible. All her life Mary had believed that God loved her. Here she was being told impossible things and being asked to trust in that love in a way she never imagined. Love stretches us sometimes and invites us to move beyond what is safe and secure. Mary surely didn't understand what it all meant, and she was surely afraid of what the future might bring, but her response comes from her deepest soul. "My wonderful God, of course I trust you. And I surrender my future to you. If this is what you want, let it be done."

THINGS TO CONSIDER
When you've finished, take a couple minutes to pray about the following. Write down a few sentences about what you experienced.

- Did you find this contemplation easy or difficult?
- What did you discover?
- Were you able to experience the story in a new way?
- What was most important to you?
- Do you trust God's love enough to surrender your life to him? Or will you choose to believe that you know better what is best for you?
- What keeps you from giving your heart to God?

Take a moment to write your reflections in your prayer journal.

CLOSING PRAYER
The grace of contemplation is deepened when we take the images and persons of our prayer with us into our daily lives. So, as you go through your week, remember Mary and what you experienced in

your time of prayer. Let the words and images be with you as you work, play, study, eat, and pray.

Now close this time of prayer by speaking to God using the prayer given here, or, better yet, your own words.

Thank you, my great and wonderful God,
for teaching me so gently of your love.
It never occurred to me
that Mary would have struggled
with the angel's message,
and that she might have been afraid and confused.
Yet I watch her respond so generously to you
and surrender her life to you.
Dear Lord, help me grow in holy freedom
so that I might give myself to you as Mary does.
Help me to say "yes."

Walking in God's presence

SUGGESTED MUSIC
"You Are Near"

PREPARATION
Find a quiet place where you will not be disturbed or distracted. Take a comfortable, relaxed sitting position. Recall that prayer is more about listening than speaking, so do not worry about what words to speak. Prepare yourself by closing your eyes and focusing on your breathing. Spend a couple of minutes sitting quietly, inhaling and exhaling deep, long breaths. Slowly become aware of God's loving presence, both around you and within you. When you're ready, continue by prayerfully reading the following reflection.

REFLECTION
O Lord, you have searched me and known me.
You know when I sit down and when I rise up;
  you discern my thoughts from far away.
You hem me in, behind and before, and lay your hand upon me.
Where can I go from your spirit? Or where can I flee from
  your presence?
If I ascend to heaven, you are there; if I make my bed in Sheol,
  you are there.

*If I take the wings of the morning and settle at the farthest lim-
    its of the sea,
even there your hand shall lead me, and your right hand shall
    hold me fast.*

    ❧ PSALM 139:1–10

Time for private prayer is an essential element for anyone intent on growing in their relationship with God and deepening their faith. But many struggle with practical questions: When during my busy life can I fit in time for prayer? How can I deal with all the distractions that pull me away from this contemplative time of my day?

These questions are real and serious. For many spiritual writers, the time of prayer and contemplation is seen as the higher calling and a more perfect way to live one's life. St. Thomas Aquinas and St. Augustine, even though they lamented the "sterility" of the contemplative life, still admitted that it was a superior way of living to that of teaching, preaching, and other "worldly" activities.

St. Ignatius of Loyola offers another perspective that might assist us in finding the balance between these seemingly polar elements of our lives. Ignatius' desire was that his followers should live and work in the heart of the world, in the very midst of people going about their lives. He did not envision his society to be like the contemplative religious orders of his time where individuals withdrew from the world.

The Ignatian vision is for a person to become a "contemplative in action." By this term, he didn't just mean that at one moment we pray, and the next moment we enter into the activity of our life. Rather, for Ignatius the activity of our life becomes the very foundation for our prayer. Our prayer flows from and through and back to the activities of our daily life. We strive to develop an attention to God's presence throughout our day and experience moments of contemplation right in the midst of our activity.

Perhaps this image will help. When we deeply love someone, we go about our daily activities carrying thoughts, memories, and feelings of our beloved in our hearts. Although the other person is not physically present, he or she is in our soul. Our mind flows back to the beloved when it has a free moment or when something reminds us of him or her. This is what Ignatius envisions for a person in love with God. We carry God with us as we go through our day, even when we are not formally at prayer.

Prayer is a relationship of our whole being, mind, and heart, with the God who loves us. Just as we surround our human relationships with symbols and rituals that assist us in keeping them alive and healthy, we must seek ways to do the same to deepen our relationship with God. At our workplace we might keep a photograph of our spouse and children on our desk as a way of keeping them present to us. We might check in at lunchtime to see how things are going. At bedtime we kiss our children good-night and say "I love you."

The habit of making God part of the fabric of our lives can be aided significantly by similar symbols and rituals. Some carry a rosary or a Sacred Heart medal. Others place a crucifix on their wall or a Bible on the nightstand. These kinds of religious symbols become anchor points in our consciousness. We can also take advantage of our daily rituals to help us. Things like getting out of bed in the morning, driving to work, sitting down to eat, walking the dog, and doing the dishes can become ritual opportunities to allow God to permeate our consciousness.

THINGS TO CONSIDER

Take some time to pray about the following questions.

- How does time for prayer fit into my day? Is it a struggle?
- How do I balance prayer with all the other things that demand my time and attention?
- How might I bring God into the routine of my day?
- What symbols and rituals would help me become more aware of God?

Take a moment to write your reflections in your prayer journal so that you can refer back to them later.

CLOSING PRAYER

For a few minutes close your eyes and imagine God's face before you. Rest in the loving gaze of your God. This is the God who loves you so much more than you know, and who wants to be more a part of your life.

When you're ready, end with the following prayer, or better, with a prayer in your own words.

God of my heart,
you know me better than I know myself
and you understand that in my heart
I want you to be more a part of my life.
Teach me, Lord, as you would patiently teach a
*   child,*
how to allow you to permeate my daily activities.
I don't think I yet understand
how much you love me and want to have me close.
Thank you, Lord, from the depths of my heart,
for your steadfast, enduring love.

Prepare the way

SUGGESTED MUSIC
"Come, Lord Jesus"

PREPARATION
Find a quiet place where you will not be disturbed or distracted. Take a comfortable, relaxed sitting position. Recall that prayer is more about listening than speaking, so do not worry about what words to speak. Prepare yourself by closing your eyes and focusing on your breathing. Slowly become mindful of God's loving presence, both around you and within you. When you're ready, continue by prayerfully reading the following reflection.

REFLECTION

> *Now the Lord said to Abram, "Go from your country and your kindred and your father's house to the land that I will show you. I will make of you a great nation, and I will bless you, and make your name great, so that you will be a blessing. I will bless those who bless you, and the one who curses you I will curse; and in you all the families of the earth shall be blessed."*
>
>   ❧ GENESIS 12:1–3

We are Advent people. We spend so much of our time in a waiting mode. Think of how many hours, days, weeks, and years you spend caught in traffic, standing in lines, looking forward to the birth of a child, or sitting beside the bed of a sick loved one. And in the final years of life, we wait for death to visit us.

The important question is not that we wait, but how we go about it. Some of us are more patient than others, not needing to control the timing and outcomes of life, but we've all experienced moments of great frustration and disappointment. We often wait with great hope and anticipation, but we can also get anxious, angry, cynical, and sometimes, downright ugly when things don't move as quickly as we'd hoped. You would think, with all the practice we have, we would grow more graceful in our waiting!

Beyond these human experiences, as people of Christian faith, we wait in hope for something bigger than ourselves. Like the Hebrew people of the Old Testament, we're waiting for the promise of our God to be fulfilled. We've heard the promise of God's kingdom of peace, justice, and equality voiced in the Scripture texts on Sunday morning. And we've known similar dreams for humanity deep in our souls. We long for the day when sin and death are no more.

The challenge of our waiting is not to become cynical, or, in the end, to despair. Many voices tell us we're foolish for believing that things will someday be different, including our own frustrating, disappointing experiences, which seem to mock our faith in God's word. We complain and grumble and flirt with giving up this way of faith. Yet in the end God helps us to hold on. The promise of God's kingdom stands clear and bold in the midst of our despair and cynicism.

It's important for us to remember that Jesus of Nazareth was a Jewish man. The Old Testament is his family history, the story of his ancestors. There is no real way to understand Jesus without understanding the context in which he lived. As a child and young man he learned from his parents of the great promise God had made to Abraham so many generations ago.

This was Jesus' spiritual background. Along with many generations of the Hebrew people, he lived his life holding on to the promise of God, waiting in hope for the fulfillment of God's word. He read the Hebrew Scripture stories that tell over and over of God's unfailing faithfulness to Israel. God brought them from slavery, safely through the sea, across the barren desert, and finally to the Promised Land. God comforted them in sorrow, encouraged them in disappointment, admonished their stubbornness, and forgave their unfaithfulness over and over again. There is no obstacle to God's word. And finally, God promised them a Savior.

How, then, can we make this journey of faith during this time between God's promise and the coming of the kingdom? Perhaps we can look to John the Baptist, one of the main characters of the Advent season, for a model. The Baptist makes it very clear that he is not the Messiah, the Promised One. He is just the herald of the glad tidings, the one announcing the coming of Christ. Like John, we strive to keep our eyes on Jesus, the One we have been waiting for.

And, like John, we might not see our labors for God's earthly kingdom or his work in our own hearts come to fruition. The work of the Spirit takes time, God's time. It is God's work, not ours. Our role is that of preparing the fertile soil in which the seed of God's word is planted, where it can flourish and grow. We are like the farmer that tills the earth, plants the seed, and then patiently waits for it to sprout.

THINGS TO CONSIDER

- Do I know how to wait in true hope?
- Have I become bitter and cynical?
- Is God's promise alive in my soul? Do I trust God to do what God says?
- Do I live the way I believe? Do I witness to the Good News?

Take a few moments to write your reflections in your prayer journal.

CLOSING PRAYER

As in previous exercises, we now end our time of reflection with a "colloquy," a heartfelt prayer in our own words, in the presence of God. We are talking to a friend. Begin with the words provided below, and then continue as your heart moves you.

God of steadfast love,
you always keep your promises.
Teach me how to prepare the way
for your coming into my heart.
Let me not get in the way of your taking flesh in this
world and in the hearts of people.
You have sent your Son, Jesus, to show us the way to
your kingdom.
With all of creation I wait in hope
for the day of his coming in glory.
Dear Lord, teach me how to wait patiently.

God with us

SUGGESTED MUSIC
"Prince of Peace"

PREPARATION
Find a quiet place where you will not be disturbed or distracted. Take a comfortable, relaxed sitting position. Prepare yourself by closing your eyes and focusing on your breathing. Spend a couple of minutes sitting quietly, inhaling and exhaling deep, long breaths. Slowly become mindful of God's loving presence, both around you and within you. Sit and take in the comfort and peace that the Lord's presence brings.

Now ask God for the grace you desire. In this exercise it is the grace to know Jesus in a deeper way and to understand the wonder and mystery of a God who takes flesh in our world.

REFLECTION
When you're ready, prayerfully read the following scripture passage.

In those days a decree went out from Emperor Augustus that all the world should be registered....Joseph also went from the town of Nazareth in Galilee to Judea, to the city of David called Bethlehem, to be registered with Mary, to whom he was engaged and who was expecting a child.

While they were there, the time came for her to deliver her child. And she gave birth to her firstborn son and wrapped him in bands of cloth, and laid him in a manger, because there was no place for them in the inn.

In that region there were shepherds living in the fields, keeping watch over their flock by night. Then an angel of the Lord stood before them, and the glory of the Lord shown around them, and they were terrified. But the angel said to them, "Do not be afraid; for see—I am bringing you Good News of great joy for all the people: to you is born this day in the city of David a Savior, who is the Messiah, the Lord. This will be a sign for you: you will find a child wrapped in bands of cloth and lying in a manger." And suddenly there was with the angel a multitude of heavenly host, praising God and saying,

"Glory to God in the highest heaven, and on earth peace among those whom he favors!"

So they went with haste and found Mary and Joseph, and the child lying in the manger. When they saw this, they made known what had been told them about this child; and all who heard it were amazed at what the shepherds told them. But Mary treasured all these words and pondered them in her heart. The shepherds returned, glorifying and praising God for all they had heard and seen, as it had been told them.

❧ LUKE 2:1–20

Now put the text down, close your eyes, and use your imagination to picture the scene with as much detail as you can. Look around to see what things look like, smell like. What sounds do you hear? Who is there? Picture the young Mary and Joseph. What are they doing? Place yourself in the scene, either as one of the characters or simply as a bystander. Begin to hear what's being said and watch the faces as the events unfold. Let the story proceed however your imagination takes you. The details of the text are not important. If something seems significant, savor it and don't hurry to move on.

Don't get discouraged if nothing seems to be happening. Sometimes God lets us feel barren and empty to teach us that it is not in our own power to experience consolation. God is very close to us at these moments when we seem unable to pray. Remember that God knows us and understands our struggle.

The act of God taking human flesh is an act of intimacy. It is a story of a God who is so in love with us that we can barely fathom it. We may feel uncomfortable with this kind of closeness to God because we feel unworthy. Furthermore, to speak of God in such human terms can seem inappropriate, if not blasphemous. And yet this is what we Christians do. The infinite, all perfect God is presented to us as a human infant, born in a lowly cattle stall to poor parents of no great importance. Such is the foolishness of God's wisdom!

In the person of Jesus, spirit and matter are at once united. The divine permeates the universe of material things in such a way that the created world is set on a course of becoming more and more divine. As the divine God takes on our humanity, so our humanity begins to take on more of God's divinity. The work and power of God's redemption of this world is set in place.

During Advent, we don't go about pretending that Jesus the Christ has yet to be born. Rather, we acknowledge our deep hunger and longing for God and the fulfillment of his promise. Christmas is not just about re-telling the Christmas story. To those who see with the eyes of faith, God continues to take on flesh for us in thousands of unexpected ways and faces.

THINGS TO CONSIDER

- Write down in your prayer journal the things you saw and heard.
- What role did you play in the story? An observer? Shepherd? Joseph? Mary?
- Did this contemplation allow you to appreciate the mystery of the incarnation in a new way?
- The grace of contemplation is deepened when we take the

images and persons of our prayer with us into our daily lives. As you go through your week, remember what you experienced in your time of prayer, and let the words and images be with you.

Take a few moments to write your reflections in your prayer journal.

CLOSING PRAYER

When you're ready, close your time of contemplation. Begin with the words provided below, and then continue as your heart moves you.

*G*reat and Infinite God,
your desire to be close to humanity overwhelms me.
Why would you even want to bother with me?
I kneel beside the manger crib to see this tiny infant,
the beauty of God in the flesh.
I sometimes don't know how to take it all in,
With Mary I try to hold it all in the quiet of my
* heart.*
Dear Lord, give me the eyes of faith
so that I might recognize you
whenever, and wherever, you take flesh for me.

Companions in Christ

SUGGESTED MUSIC
"Pilgrim Companions"

PREPARATION
Find a quiet place where you will not be disturbed or distracted. Take a comfortable, relaxed sitting position. Spend a couple minutes sitting quietly, inhaling and exhaling deep, long breaths. There's no need to rush. Slowly become mindful of God's presence, both around you and within you. Breathe in the comfort and peace God's loving presence brings. When you're ready, continue by prayerfully reading the following reflection.

REFLECTION
With great kindness, God has bestowed an abundance of grace on you through these past weeks. This exercise does not present new material for reflection, but rather invites you to go back over the reflections you have already done in order to savor the powerful moments of grace that have been given you. You're invited in this exercise to recall the graces you've been given, to relish them and find even more goodness in them. In the life of the spirit, savoring any grace or consolation that's been given us is never a waste of time.

The first step is to go back and look at what you have written in your prayer journal for each of the previous exercises. Pay special attention to the notes you made at the end of each exercise. This is where you tried to put into words that exercise's special grace for you. In the presence of God read through what you wrote. Put a mark next to the entries that seem to be the most important, the ones that hold the most significance for you, and the ones that seem to bring you the most joy and peace.

The entries you've marked are the ones that you should spend more time with. For now, pick one of them. Remember back to that moment in the previous exercise and recall what it felt like. What was so significant about it? Why did it mean so much to you? Embrace it and savor it. Don't feel compelled to rush and move forward, even if you spend the rest of your prayer time with this one grace. Allow yourself the opportunity to bathe in God's infinite love and mercy. There's no need to figure anything out or draw a conclusion. Just be with God in the moment.

Growing in the life of the Spirit is really about falling in love. It's about a personal relationship with Jesus. It's also, of course, about doctrines, moral principles, and being able to quote Scripture, but the first step is the encounter with Christ. The fact is, the almighty and infinite God, the Creator of this vast universe, is in love with you and hopes that you will fall in love with him. At their core, these exercises are about spending time with and getting to know God, to see him in our daily lives, and to hear him speak to us in our hearts and minds.

> *Nothing is more practical than finding God, that is, than falling in love in a quite absolute, final way.*
>
> *What you are in love with, what seizes your imagination, will affect everything. It will decide what will get you out of bed in the morning, what you will do with your evenings, how you will spend your weekends, what you read, who you know, what breaks your heart, and what amazes you with joy and gratitude.*

Fall in love, stay in love, and it will decide everything.

🍂 PEDRO ARRUPE, SJ, SUPERIOR GENERAL OF THE
SOCIETY OF JESUS, 1961–1984

There is nothing like a teenager who falls in love for the first time. Their whole day revolves around the other person. They lose track of time and spend hours on the phone just talking about nothing. All they desire is to be in each other's presence. As we get a little older, we realize that falling in love might mean that we'll have to change our way of life, reveal ourselves to the other person in unaccustomed ways, allowing the other person to experience our selfishness and sinfulness. As we lose our innocence, falling in love takes more time.

This process of falling in love is what God has been doing within you through these exercises. Through grace God has been revealed to you and opened your heart to fuller love. God has been stretching your heart so that you can receive more love, and little by little, opening up the possibility that you will fall in love with him, too.

There are very few people who realize what God would make of them if they abandoned themselves into his hands, and let themselves be formed by his grace.

🍂 ST. IGNATIUS OF LOYOLA

We are not alone on our journey to let God's love transform us. We have many other travelers to stand with, men and women who have the same dreams, experience the same struggles, and hold on to the same hopeful promise. When we are discouraged, the faith of those other travelers can raise us up and give us the strength and desire to continue. God provides such pilgrims as a gift to us.

THINGS TO CONSIDER
Simply allow yourself to bask in the warmth of God's goodness and grace. Write anything of significance in your prayer journal.

CLOSING PRAYER

Close your eyes and imagine God's face before you, the God who is so proud of you and takes such great delight in you. Allow yourself to soak up God's love, like basking in the warmth and light of the sun. When you feel ready, end with the following prayer, or better, with a prayer in your own words.

*D*ear God, Lord of Love,
    I sit here feeling nervous before the gaze of your love.
    I'm not accustomed to letting you look at me in this
        way.
    The power and depth of your love take my breath
        away.
    Forgive me if I'm not yet able to give myself to you
        completely,
    not yet able to fall in love with you.
    Make up for what is lacking in my desire, Lord.
    Let the fire of your love transform me.

Walking with Jesus

SUGGESTED MUSIC
"We Will Journey in Faith"

PREPARATION
Remember that prayer is more about listening than about having the right words to say. We listen better when our souls are quiet and receptive. Close your eyes and focus your attention on your breathing. Take several long and slow deep breaths. Imagine that you are breathing in the goodness of God's Spirit, and breathing out all that troubles you. Sit quietly in the presence of the God who loves you beyond what you could ever understand. Now ask for the grace you desire. In this exercise it is the grace to become aware of your desires, your hungers, and how they influence the good or bad choices you make. When you're ready, continue by prayerfully reading the following reflection.

REFLECTION
> *Blessed are the poor in spirit,*
> *for theirs is the kingdom of heaven.*
> *Blessed are those who mourn,*
> *for they will be comforted.*
> *Blessed are the meek,*
> *for they will inherit the earth.*

Blessed are the peacemakers,
for they will be called children of God.
❧ MATTHEW 5:3–5, 9

We began these spiritual exercises by reflecting on our desires, those deep hungers that abide in our soul. It is through this soulful hunger that God leads us into deeper intimacy. But it's also important to recognize that our desires can sometimes take us away from God by seducing us to choose things that lead to pride and independence from God, things that can, in the end, separate us from our union with Christ.

At any moment, we are being pulled in one direction by our culture of consumerism and power, and at the same time being drawn by the gentle force of grace toward a freedom that allows us in all things to choose God. The attraction of riches, pride, and prestige is powerful. We feel secure and in charge of our lives through our accomplishments and the material things with which we surround ourselves. The only problem with this is that we begin to think of ourselves as independent from God. We can either choose a life that is selfish and egotistical, or live in dependence on God, surrendering our own desires into God's hands.

God has a dream for us, for all humanity. Jesus of Nazareth calls it the kingdom of God. The gospel accounts are filled with parables and lessons in which Jesus describes what the kingdom of God is like. This kingdom of peace, justice, and beauty is being built among us through the power of Jesus Christ. How could we not choose such a dream? Of course we want peace, justice, and the fullness of joy!

But the challenge comes not in choosing the dream, but rather in the strategy used by Christ to bring the kingdom into being. His strategy is to bring about peace and justice by standing alongside those who are outcasts, marginalized, poor, and powerless. That's the hard part.

Jesus doesn't embrace this strategy just because it's the harder thing to do, but because in God's kingdom there are no outcasts, no marginalized, no poor, no oppressed. Everyone is welcome at the table, not just the rich and the powerful. Instinctively none of us would choose poverty over riches, humility over honor. But through Christ, our hearts are transformed to see through his eyes and to understand that when we gather at his table, all are welcome, not just the wealthy and honorable. The dream of God's kingdom is about love. Love is at the heart of it.

In his *Spiritual Exercises*, Ignatius invites a person to "consider Christ our Lord standing "in a lowly place."[4] We envision ourselves standing there with Christ among the lowly ones, those whom this world rejects and considers inferior. Jesus embraces humility as a way to be in solidarity with those who are embarrassed about their lives. He embraces poverty because it leads to solidarity with the poor and helpless. He rejects earthly honor because it separates him from those who are looked upon as having no status or dignity. We are invited to stand with Christ in poverty, humility, and meekness because this is his strategy to bring the dream of God's kingdom.

When we allow ourselves to stand with Jesus, we allow our hearts to be broken by the same things that break his heart. We allow the poor, the outcast, the forgotten and helpless to affect us, to remind us of our own poverty and helplessness. We receive from them the gift they have for us, and we become one with them. The kingdom of God becomes a reality for us and for them. We've not just preached the message, but we've allowed ourselves to become the message of God's kingdom.

THINGS TO CONSIDER

- Reflect on your manner of living and the choices you've made.
- How does the culture of consumerism play out in your life?
- Do you need things to feel important or good about yourself?
- Do you allow yourself to know the poor and the outcast?
- Who are the marginalized in your life?

- Do you allow your heart to be broken by the sorrow of others?

Take a few moments to write your reflections in your prayer journal.

CLOSING PRAYER

In the presence of Jesus, let him share with you God's dream for humanity. Listen to him and allow your heart to be filled with a desire to share in this dream. When you're ready, continue with the following prayer, or better, with a prayer in your own words.

God of great Kindness,
Fill my heart with love for your least ones.
I want to share your dream
and stand with Jesus in that lowly place
*   called the kingdom of God.*
I am so far from embracing poverty and humility,
*   but I pray that you may gently teach me.*
Thank you for loving me so much
*   and for showing me*
the tender compassion of God.

Temptation in the desert

SUGGESTED MUSIC

"Give Us Faith, Lord"

PREPARATION

Close your eyes and focus your attention on your breathing. Take several long and slow deep breaths. Imagine that you are breathing in the goodness of God's Spirit, and breathing out all that troubles you. Sit quietly for a moment in the presence of the loving God. Then ask for the grace you desire. In this exercise it is the grace to know Jesus more intimately as he struggles to follow God's call. When you're ready, continue with the reflection.

REFLECTION

In this exercise we'll place ourselves with Jesus at the beginning of his public ministry. We'll again use a kind of prayer that St. Ignatius calls "contemplation." Using the power of our imagination, we enter a Scripture passage, not only to understand it, but beyond that, to actually experience it in our hearts. This kind of prayer takes the story beyond its surface details and allows the story to come alive for us. We become participants.

We know from the gospel stories that Jesus was baptized by John the Baptist in the Jordan River and was then led by God's Spirit into the desert to prepare for his ministry. There Jesus is tempted by the Evil One. We will watch with admiration as he struggles to stay true to his identity as the servant of God who brings the good news that the poor and weak are blessed in God's eyes.

Slowly read the Scripture account through once.

Then Jesus was led up by the Spirit into the wilderness to be tempted by the devil. He fasted forty days and forty nights, and afterwards he was famished. The tempter came and said to him, "If you are the Son of God, command these stones to become loaves of bread." But he answered, "It is written, 'One does not live by bread alone, but by every word that comes from the mouth of God.'"

Then the devil took him to the holy city and placed him on the pinnacle of the temple, saying to him, "If you are the Son of God, throw yourself down; for it is written, 'He will command his angels concerning you,' and 'On their hands they will bear you up, so that you will not dash your foot against a stone.'" Jesus said to him, "Again it is written, 'Do not put the Lord your God to the test.'"

Again, the devil took him to a very high mountain and showed him all the kingdoms of the world and their splendor; and he said to him, "All these I will give you, if you fall down and worship me." Jesus said to him, "Away with you, Satan! For it is written, 'Worship the Lord your God, and serve only him.'" Then the devil left him, and suddenly angels came and waited on him.

✸ MATTHEW 4:1–11

Now put the text down, close your eyes, and use your imagination to picture the scene with as much detail as you can. Imagine being in the desert. What does it look like? Smell like? What is the air like? Imagine Jesus alone. What is he doing and feeling? Begin to hear what's being said, and watch as the events unfold. Let the story proceed in whatever way your imagination takes you. The details of the text are not important. Try to spend about thirty minutes with this part. If you spend all your time with it, don't feel that you need to move on. But when you're ready, or at your next prayer time, continue with the reflection.

Jesus' experience of these desert temptations might seem disconnected from our own struggles. After all, have we ever been offered all the kingdoms of the world if we'd only bow down and worship the Evil One? Or been tempted to throw ourselves off a high tower to test God's care? At their very heart, these temptations are about pride and arrogance. As the serpent did with Adam and Eve, the Evil One likes to confuse our thinking about who we really are. We're lured by the dream of thinking that we can be like God, with knowledge of good and evil, controlling the timing and outcome of our lives.

The truth of our lives is that we are not God, but creatures, the work of God's hands. Our very existence is bestowed on us as pure gift. Ultimately we've had nothing to say or do about the miracle of our own birth. We don't control the movement of the stars or the number of days we walk this earth. As was true for Jesus, our glory as creatures lies in our being the beloved of God. Receiving the generosity of his love is our joy. The key is self-acceptance, embracing the glory of who we are but not trying to be something we are not.

We live in pride when we think we've somehow earned the good things in our lives. We live in arrogance when we think we're better than others because of what we've accomplished, how much wealth we've accumulated, or the power we possess. All these things can be taken from us in an instant and are not ours in the first place.

Sometimes the depth of our spiritual hunger can make us desperate. We hate the empty hole in our soul and look for ways to fill it. Unfortunately, the things we choose to fill our hunger are not always good for us. Our contemporary society offers many compelling distractions. For some, accumulating material possessions is an attempt to fill the hunger of the soul. Others will use work, alcohol, medications, sex, or food to deaden the ache in their soul. Rather than depending on God to fill us, we sometimes end up choosing only temporary, hurtful solutions.

THINGS TO CONSIDER

- What was most significant for you? What did you see, feel, hear?
- What did you learn about Jesus?
- Did you experience consolation, desolation, or something in between?
- Do you try to be aware of your inner hunger? Do you treat it with respect and reverence?
- Do you try to numb the hunger you feel in unhealthy, unholy ways?

Take a few moments to write your reflections in your prayer journal.

CLOSING PRAYER

Finally, speak to God using the prayer given here, or, better yet, pray in your own words.

*K*ind and generous God,
it is comforting to be with Jesus in his humanity
as he is tempted to forget who he is
and what his purpose is.
I am very aware of my pride and arrogance
and how I try to use your gifts
to attract attention to myself
*   or fill the empty place in my soul.*
Teach me, dear Lord, to be ever grateful.
Teach me how to receive your gifts with open arms
ever trusting that you will always provide
*   just what I need to fill my hunger.*

The harvest is plenty

SUGGESTED MUSIC
"Come with Me into the Fields"

PREPARATION
Find a quiet place where you will not be distracted. Close your eyes and focus on your breathing. Sit quietly as you become aware of God's loving presence. After a few moments, ask for the grace to know Jesus more intimately. The more time we spend with him, the more we begin to know him. The more we know him, the more we are drawn to love him. When you feel ready, continue with the reflection.

REFLECTION
For this exercise, we will again use the prayer of contemplation. We'll watch Jesus walk along the shore of the Sea of Galilee as he happens upon some fishermen. It's a simple story and one very familiar to us. However, it has profound meaning for us as we get to know Jesus. It's not just a story about some people that lived many centuries ago. Begin by reading through the Scripture once.

As Jesus passed along the Sea of Galilee, he saw Simon and his brother Andrew casting a net into the sea—for they were fishermen. And Jesus said to them, "Follow me and I will make you fish for people." And immediately they left their nets and followed him. As he went a little farther, he saw James son of Zebedee and his brother John, who were in their boat mending the nets. Immediately he called them; and they left their father Zebedee in the boat with the hired men, and followed him.

❧ MARK 1:16–20

Now put down the text, close your eyes, walk through the story as if you are there on the shore. Let the story unfold in whatever way your imagination takes you. The details of the text are not important. This is your story and it can go however you imagine it. God's Spirit will take your heart just where it needs to go. Don't get discouraged if nothing seems to be happening or if you feel distracted. Sometimes God lets us feel barren and empty to help us realize that it is not in our own power to experience consolation. If this happens during your prayer, simply ask God again for what you desire. There's no need to rush. If you spend all your prayer time on this part, that's fine.

When you finish, in order to deepen the contemplation, prayerfully read the following reflection.

Why would they do it? These fishermen, cleaning their boats and mending their nets after a long night, spot a stranger walking toward them on the beach. At first they don't pay much attention. But when he gets close, he greets them and strikes up a conversation. Before they know it, he's asking them to come along with him. And amazingly, they go, leaving behind the only world they've ever known.

Although many details of the story were surely left out of the gospel account, the core of the story is still there. Jesus invited the fishermen to follow him and they went with him. It's hard for us to imagine walking away from our livelihood and following a stranger. What could be so compelling about Jesus to convince them to do such a thing? Perhaps it was something in his voice, in his eyes, that reached into that deep-down hunger in their souls and offered them something they never thought possible.

As I listen to Jesus' invitation, I can hear the desire in his voice. "Come, follow me." It's not just that he wants disciples; he needs companionship, my companionship, as he proclaims the good news of God's kingdom. He must know that the path ahead will not be easy, that it will mean loneliness, sleepless nights, and even rejection. He depends on the companionship, encouragement, and comfort of those who are willing to walk with him.

But why would he want me? He has his mission from God. But me, I'm just a fisherman and I don't have eloquent words to speak or teach. I don't have much education. And God knows I've done some pretty bad things for which I'm terribly ashamed. And yet, here he is, looking at me, asking me to be his companion. His eyes seem to look right into my soul.

What is it that keeps me from going with him? Am I afraid to give up the security of my life? Or could it be that I resist walking into an unknown future that can take me to places that are unfamiliar and unsafe? Perhaps I'm just stuck, not willing to take a leap of faith into God's hands. Or maybe I think his message is just some kind of idealistic propaganda that could never solve the problems of the real world.

Just as those first disciples experienced, following Jesus means our hearts must be transformed, and it is love that changes us. They experienced a profound conversion as the result of meeting Jesus and getting to know him. Little by little, they assimilated the values that they admire in him and tried to emulate the way he lived. When they truly fell in love, it changed them in profound ways.

THINGS TO CONSIDER

- What did I experience in this contemplation? What was most significant?
- What did I learn about Jesus?
- Did I experience consolation, desolation, or something in between?
- What would be so compelling for me that I would choose to follow Jesus? Did I feel generous or hesitant or afraid? Why?

Write anything that seems significant in your prayer journal.

CLOSING PRAYER

Now take some time to speak to God using the prayer given here, or, better yet, pray in your own words.

*G*ood and gentle Lord Jesus,
I listen to your invitation and I am afraid.
I'm afraid of what might happen if I say "yes."
And yet when I look into your eyes,
I see how much you hope
  that I will come along.
I will need your help to respond wholeheartedly.
Please make up for whatever
  is lacking in my desire.
Teach me how to say "yes."

We want to see Jesus

SUGGESTED MUSIC
"Only This I Want"

PREPARATION
Find a quiet place where you won't be disturbed. Begin by closing your eyes and focusing on your breathing. Inhale slowly and deeply while imagining that the presence of God is filling you. Then exhale slowly as you release any anxiety and tension. Ask for the grace to know Jesus more intimately. When you're ready, continue with the following reflection.

REFLECTION
In this exercise we're going to listen to our teacher Jesus, and let his words thrill us and comfort us. We'll again use the prayer of contemplation to help us enter into the gospel story. We'll imagine ourselves sitting with the crowds on the hillside on a magnificent summer day, all of us eager to hear what he might have to say to us today. Never have we heard anyone else speak like this. We'll experience this story as if it's happening to us right here and now. Take the Scripture line by line and let the scene unfold in your own time. There's no need to rush forward.

When Jesus saw the crowds, he went up the mountain; and after
he sat down, his disciples came to him. Then he began to speak,
and taught them, saying:

"Blessed are the poor in spirit,
for theirs is the kingdom of heaven.
Blessed are those who mourn,
for they will be comforted.
Blessed are the meek,
for they will inherit the earth.
Blessed are those who hunger and thirst
for righteousness, for they will be filled.
Blessed are the merciful,
for they will receive mercy.
Blessed are the pure in heart,
for they will see God.
Blessed are the peacemakers,
for they will be called children of God.
Blessed are those who are persecuted for righteousness' sake, for
theirs is the kingdom of heaven.
Blessed are you when people revile you and persecute you and
utter all kinds of evil against you falsely on my account. Re-
joice and be glad, for your reward is great in heaven."

  ❧ MATTHEW 5:1–12

As a way of deepening the contemplation, slowly read through the following reflection. Take note of anything that strikes you as significant.

When we love someone, we care about what they have to say. We're willing to take the time to listen to what's important to them, what gives them joy and inspires them. And we don't just listen to the words. We let the words penetrate our hearts and change us. We can imagine Jesus looking out at the faces of these people, asking himself, "What do their hearts need to hear?" He can see their ache and longing, their deep down hunger for God, their pain. Many of them are troubled souls that are empty of hope. Some are in mourning over the death of a loved one or a deep disappointment. There are those who have been deeply hurt by those who've judged them to be unfit, unacceptable, and unworthy of love.

And so Jesus begins to speak to their souls and tells them that all this ache and longing makes a person blessed. Many of them probably expected him to preach about what they need to do to become holy. But he surprises them by telling them that they're already holy and blessed and beloved in God's eyes. What a message of hope and freedom this is! Holiness is not about how many prayers I say or how generous I am. It's about being loved and embraced in my poverty, meekness, and hunger. It's about being pure of heart and heralds of peace. And it's about one's willingness to bear insult and rejection for the sake of God's kingdom. This is truly good news.

We might find ourselves resisting some of the things we hear in Jesus' teaching. This is a radical new way of thinking and of looking at life. Are we ready to embrace the mind of Jesus, our friend and brother? Like some of the disciples we may be thinking that this man has to get a more realistic grasp on life. How could he really be serious to count anyone fortunate and blessed who is grieving, meek, or persecuted? Maybe we have a hard time imagining ourselves as poor, meek, or pure of heart.

That crowd on the side of the hill surely didn't understand all that Jesus' words meant. But they did sense in his voice a hope that filled them with profound happiness. The heart of the Beatitudes is that we are blessed when we depend on God rather than on ourselves, our talents, our natural gifts, or financial resources. Happiness is found in looking at the world in a new way, Christ's way, where we are the empty vessels that God fills with an abundance of joy.

The freedom of Jesus' message is that we don't have to become something other than we are to be holy and blessed. Favor with God is not found only in times of joy, or being a success, or when we have our lives figured out and under control. It is in being true to ourselves that we are blessed by God.

THINGS TO CONSIDER

- What was most significant for me in this exercise?
- What was I feeling? Did I experience consolation? Or was I restless and uncomfortable? Why might this be so?
- What in Jesus' teaching do I resist? What seems out of sync with my view of the world?

Take a moment to write your reflections in your prayer journal.

CLOSING PRAYER

Now take some time to speak to God using the prayer given here, or, better yet, pray in your own words.

*D*earest Lord Jesus,
I am coming to love and admire you
more and more each day.
I don't always understand your words
but I feel great comfort in them
and great freedom.
You remind me
that I don't have to earn God's blessing
but that holiness lies
in being myself before God.
I often feel that I am not yet ready
to be your disciple,
yet you call me to your side.
Help me to respond with all my heart.

Lord, make me whole

SUGGESTED MUSIC
"See the Lilies"

PREPARATION

Begin this exercise by finding a quiet place where you won't be disturbed. Spend a few moments centering yourself, taking several slow, deep breaths and focusing on the presence of God in you and around you. Ask for the grace to come to know Jesus more intimately, to understand his mind and heart, and to love him more completely. When you're ready, continue with the following reflection.

REFLECTION

Today we watch Jesus as he responds with great compassion to a man who cries out for healing. As you read the gospel account use the imaginative prayer of contemplation to enter more deeply into the story. The goal is to allow the scene to become real, as if it were happening right before you. Take the Scripture line by line as you watch the faces and hear what's being said. Let the scene unfold in your imagination. There's no need to rush.

> *As he approached Jericho, a blind man was sitting by the roadside begging. When he heard a crowd going by, he asked what*

was happening. They told him, "Jesus of Nazareth is passing by." Then he shouted, "Jesus, Son of David, have mercy on me!" Those who were in front sternly ordered him to be quiet; but he shouted even more loudly, "Son of David, have mercy on me!" Jesus stood still and ordered the man to be brought to him; and when he came near, he asked him, "What do you want me to do for you?" He said, "Lord, let me see again." Jesus said to him, "Receive your sight; your faith has saved you." Immediately he regained his sight and followed him, glorifying God; and all the people, when they saw it, praised God.

❧ LUKE 18:35–43

When you finish, as a way of deepening the contemplation, prayerfully read the following reflection. Take note of anything that strikes you as significant.

It is not easy to admit that we are flawed. We are often embarrassed by our inadequacies, whether it be a physical flaw, a mental disorder, or even a spiritual wound. Life is hard and none of us escapes some form of brokenness. And there are poignant moments when we'd like to cry out to God, "Lord, make me whole again!" We'd like to hope that healing is possible but are often told that we should be more realistic and just keep quiet.

The blind man in the gospel story refuses to be silenced by the crowd around him. One can only imagine their taunting: "Why would he pay any attention to you? Look at your miserable life! Do you really believe that he'd stop to talk with you?" Behind the blind man's persistence is a deep faith that Jesus would listen to his pleas.

Sometimes, however, we just don't want to be healed. We'd rather hold on to the spiritual and emotional hurt we carry for the times we were verbally abused as children, or the abandonment we felt when our spouse walked out on our marriage, or the anger we felt when we were betrayed by a close friend.

The first step to healing is realizing how much we are loved. It is so moving to watch how Jesus treats those who are disfigured and broken. Jesus pays special attention to them and treats them with amazing reverence. He tells the crowd to bring the blind man to him. One can imagine the kindness with which Jesus looks at the man. He doesn't focus on the man's infirmity but simply asks him what he wants. It's such a reverent, loving thing to do. He never blames the man for his blindness, even though in his culture this kind of physical infirmity was seen as a punishment from God for some sinful transgression. Healing comes to us when we stop blaming ourselves for the bad things that happen to us.

When God reaches out with healing grace, it is not just for the sake of making us whole. God heals us from something so that we might be able to extend that same healing to the world beyond us. The kindness and compassion of Jesus embrace the blind man so that he in turn may become kind and compassionate toward others.

In our living we will come across people who are in need of God's compassion and healing mercy. Before they can hear about God, they need someone to speak words of encouragement, a friend to hear the hurt they are carrying, or a faith pilgrim who's willing to share their own journey of faith. Great healing can come in sharing our hurts with someone who has also known pain, hurt, and misfortune. Our willingness to pass on the compassion of God is the way we give thanks for the healing that's come to us.

THINGS TO CONSIDER

- What happened during my prayer? What surprised me most? What was most important?
- What did I come to know about Jesus?
- What hurts do I hold inside me? What anger am I unwilling to let go of?
- What painful memories need the healing of God's love and acceptance?
- How do I treat those who are disfigured, distasteful, or repulsive?
- Does my discomfort keep me from responding with compassion?

Take a moment to write your reflections in your prayer journal.

CLOSING PRAYER

Close your eyes and imagine yourself in the presence of Jesus. Let him look at you with great love and kindness. When you're ready, continue with the following prayer, or with a prayer in your own words. Speak to God as a friend speaks to a friend.

Dear, gentle Jesus,
my faith is tender.
I come to you
needing to know that you love me.
Only in your presence can I find the courage
to look at my brokenness
and to see myself as you see me.
Help me to let the power of your love
reach into those painful places in my heart
that are bruised and need healing.
Let me rest for a moment
in the comfort of your embrace.

Glad tidings for the poor

SUGGESTED MUSIC
"I Found the Treasure"

PREPARATION

Following the pattern of past exercises, find a quiet place and spend a few moments centering yourself. Close your eyes and take several slow, deep breaths. Imagine that you are breathing the Spirit of God into yourself. Ask for the grace to make your relationship with Christ the first priority in your life. When you're ready, prayerfully read through the following reflection.

REFLECTION

Our relationship with Jesus Christ is like any of our human relationships. It needs time and attention on our part to keep it healthy and growing. The seed of faith that's been planted in our soul has begun to grow into a flourishing tree, but it needs cultivating, fertilizing, and pruning to help it bear fruit. And so we continue with these exercises to help us do that in a structured way.

It's important that we take the time to become aware of how we are letting God's word grow in us. In his *Spiritual Exercises*, St. Ignatius encourages us to begin a daily ritual he calls the "examination of conscience." He considered this to be perhaps the single most important spiritual exercise that one can do. Though the "examen" has often been presented as a method of counting our moral shortcomings, Ignatius' purpose is much broader and much more positive. In his mind, the purpose of the examen is to become aware of God's presence in the concrete circumstances of our lives, to look at where God reveals himself during our daily activities.

Here is how the examination works:

- Begin by placing yourself in the presence of God, who loves you unconditionally.
- Thank God for the good things of your day. These are often simple things, but some days, may be profoundly important.
- Reflect on the events of your day and ask yourself what was important. Where did you find God?
- Pay attention to where you may have resisted God's grace.
- Finally, speak to God intimately, as a friend, sharing your day and asking for the grace of faith, hope, and love.

Take ten to fifteen minutes now to do the examination yourself. It's a simple process and you can adapt it to your own needs. When you're ready, continue with the reflection.

Our faith is about a real, living, growing relationship with Jesus. All the rest—the history and doctrine, the understanding of sacraments and grace, the knowledge of Scripture—is quite meaningless if we are not growing in intimacy with Christ. When we give witness to our faith, the most powerful message is our own growing relationship with Jesus and our sincere desire to grow closer to him.

When he came to Nazareth, where he had been brought up, he went to the synagogue on the Sabbath day, as was his custom. He stood up to read, and the scroll of the prophet Isaiah was given to him. He unrolled the scroll and found the place where it was written:
"The Spirit of the Lord is upon me,
because he has anointed me
to bring good news to the poor.

He has sent me to proclaim release to the captives
and recovery of sight to the blind,
to let the oppressed go free,
to proclaim the year of the Lord's favor."
And he rolled up the scroll, gave it back to the attendant,
and sat down. The eyes of all in the synagogue were fixed on
him. Then he began to say to them, "Today this Scripture has
been fulfilled in your hearing." All spoke well of him and were
amazed at the gracious words that came from his mouth. They
said, "Is not this Joseph's son?"

❧ LUKE 4:16–22

This passage describes Jesus' mission. As his companions and disciples, it is also our mission. God has anointed us to be the heralds of glad tidings to the poor, to bring sight to the blind, comfort to those in sorrow, and liberty to those imprisoned. But the good news we announce is not something written in a book. It's something we've experienced in our own lives, in our own hearts. We are coming to know Jesus and are growing in intimacy with him. We've experienced the Good News that he brings because we ourselves have been blind, poor, and imprisoned.

As with Jesus, there may be times when others don't receive what we teach with open hearts. Our students might doubt us, just as people doubted Jesus. Our success or failure as teachers does not depend wholly on our abilities. Sometimes our words fall on fertile soil. Other times they fall on rocky ground. Jesus is the one in charge and has his own time and place for the seed to take root in people's hearts. Our mission is to offer ourselves, with open hearts for ministry, bearing witness to the God we've come to know and love.

THINGS TO CONSIDER
- Did I find the examination of conscience helpful?
- How can I make it into something that helps me grow closer to Christ?

- How can I incorporate the examination of conscience into my daily life?

Spend a couple of minutes writing your reflections in your prayer journal.

CLOSING PRAYER

As in previous exercises, we now end our time of reflection with a colloquy, a heartfelt prayer, in one's own words, in the presence of God. It should be like a friend talking to a friend. Begin with the words provided below, and then continue as your heart may move you.

Dearest Lord Jesus,
You know my heart and its ways.
You know that my deepest desire
is to be close to you,
but sometimes I just don't take the time
to pay attention to you in my life.
When you are alive in my life
I know that I am a better witness
to the glad tidings that you bring.
Help me to be a herald of your good news
to bring light where there is darkness,
sight where there is blindness,
hope where there is despair,
and freedom where there are prisons.

Mercy for all

SUGGESTED MUSIC
"God of Love"

PREPARATION
After you find a quiet place, close your eyes and breathe slowly and deeply. Concentrate on your breathing and imagine that you are taking in God's kindness and beauty as you breathe out all that is dark and stressful. Ask for the grace to receive God's healing mercy into your soul.

REFLECTION
In this exercise, we simply want to rest in the loving embrace of God's unbounded mercy. We might carry in our hearts the image of God embracing us and offering us unlimited forgiveness. We're again going to use the Ignatian method of contemplative prayer to enter into a gospel story where Jesus extends God's healing mercy to a woman known to be a great sinner. Those present at the table with Jesus are shocked at his response to the woman.

Read through the gospel account once to understand the details of the story. Once you've done this, close your eyes and imagine yourself in the house of the Pharisee where Jesus and others have gathered around a table. Imagine what the room looks like. See the people, how they are dressed and where they are seated. In your own way and your own time, let the story unfold before you. The details are not as important as allowing yourself to experience the interaction as if it's really happening to you. Be one of the characters in the story and let yourself feel what's being said and done.

> *One of the Pharisees asked Jesus to eat with him, and he went into the Pharisee's house and took his place at the table. A woman in the city, who was a sinner, having learned that he was eating in the Pharisee's house, brought an alabaster jar of ointment. She stood behind him at his feet, weeping, and began to bathe his feet with her tears and to dry them with her hair. Then she continued kissing his feet and anointing them with the ointment. When the Pharisee who had invited him saw it, he said to himself, "If this man were a prophet, he would have known who and what kind of woman this is who is touching him—that she is a sinner." Jesus spoke up and said to him, "Simon, I have something to say to you." "Teacher," he replied, "speak." "Do you see this woman? I entered your house; you gave me no water for my feet, but she has bathed my feet with her tears and dried them with her hair. You gave me no kiss, but from the time I came in, she has not stopped kissing my feet. You did not anoint my head with oil, but she has anointed my feet with ointment. Therefore, I tell you, her sins, which were many, have been forgiven; she has shown great love. But the one to whom little is forgiven, loves little." Then he said to her, "Your sins are forgiven. Your faith has saved you; go in peace."*

> ❧ LUKE 7:36–40, 44–50

For this woman this was certainly one of life's most embarrassing moments. She must have felt so utterly ashamed and humiliated, and yet is courageous enough to kneel before Jesus. How she was allowed to enter the Pharisee's house in the first place is hard to imagine. And here she is washing Jesus' feet with her tears. What an amazing act of contrition it was!

Jesus' reaction to the woman is startling and unexpected. He is so tender with her. In an amazingly kind gesture of compassion, he shifts the focus away from the woman and toward the Pharisee who questions his actions. Surprisingly, he doesn't chastise the woman for her sinfulness; but rather, he chastises the Pharisee for his arrogance in judging her actions and judging Jesus himself for receiving her act of contrition. Sometimes we hear the voice of the Pharisee in our hearts because we just can't understand a God who is so generous with his mercy.

In this story Jesus reveals for us the heart of God, who never turns us away or abandons us, even in our sin. Without hesitation God welcomes us with open arms and rejoices that we've come back home. It's not important to God that we count up our sins or enumerate the details. The hardest part for us is overcoming our shame and humbly asking God for forgiveness.

We, not God, are the ones who separate ourselves from his love. We are the ones who choose to live apart from God. But as soon as we turn back toward God, he is there waiting for us. It is not our own efforts, but rather God's unbounded love and mercy, that will transform us from sinner to saint.

THINGS TO CONSIDER

- What happened during your time of contemplation? What did you experience? What did you hear or see in the contemplation that you've never noticed before?
- Was this a time of consolation, desolation, or something in between for you?
- What area of your sinfulness do you allow to separate yourself from God? Of what are you most ashamed? Is there anything that you have a hard time believing that God would forgive?

Take some time to write your reflections in your prayer journal.

CLOSING PRAYER

As in previous exercises, we now end our time of reflection with a
colloquy, a heartfelt prayer, in one's own words. This should be like
a friend talking to a friend. Begin with the words provided below,
and then continue as your heart moves you. Ask God for what you
desire.

Dearest, most merciful Jesus,
I am overwhelmed
*   with the depth of your love for me.*
Sometimes I stay away
because it's hard for me to believe
*   that you would welcome me in my sin.*
Forgive my arrogance in not trusting your love.
I'm so grateful, Lord,
that you're willing to welcome me
back home.
Let me never judge my brothers and sisters.
May I always be ready
to embrace them with forgiveness
*   and extend to them*
the abundance of your mercy.

Community of love

SUGGESTED MUSIC
"Litany of Saints"

PREPARATION

Begin by closing your eyes and breathing deeply for a few moments as a way of centering yourself. Become aware that you are surrounded by the loving presence of God, who is there to guide you and nurture you. Ask for the grace to become aware of the community of holy men and women who travel beside you in faith. When you're ready, continue by prayerfully reading the following reflection.

REFLECTION

> *They devoted themselves to the apostles' teaching and fellowship, to the breaking of bread and the prayers. Awe came upon everyone, because many wonders and signs were being done by the apostles. All who believed were together and had things in common; they would sell their possessions and goods and distribute the proceeds to all, as any had need.*
>
> ꙮ ACTS 2:42-45

As Jesus begins his public ministry he gathers around himself a group of friends to share his hope and dream for the kingdom of God. They travel the roads of Galilee together, sharing both successes and failures. One can easily imagine the many meals they must have shared, the lively discussions about God, and the mutual support they were able to give each other. Like us, they walked side by side with other men and women who were their hope and inspiration. Many times our faith is born from the lives of those around us, extraordinary, but sometimes very ordinary, people who live their lives simply and sincerely in the light of God's grace.

The name "saints" has often been used in the history of the Church to address the members of the living community of believers. For example, Paul addresses his letter to the "saints who are in Ephesus" or "the saints and faithful brothers and sisters in Christ in Colossae." This seems to reinforce an understanding in the early Church that sainthood and holiness were not things a person earned, but were rather a gift from God bestowed on all the baptized.

Our holiness lies in our common baptism into the Body of Christ. We are brothers and sisters because we have all been marked with the sign of Christ and have become heirs of the glory of his resurrection. While we do not earn our kinship in the Body of Christ, we strive to live in a way that is authentic to our identity as brothers and sisters. We offer each other encouragement, inspiration, and companionship. We give comfort to those in sorrow, hope to those in despair, faith to those who stumble, and show special care for the poor among us.

We've each been given unique gifts to offer to our brothers and sisters. Sometimes our gifts are apparent and public, such as preaching, singing, teaching, and serving at the eucharistic table. And sometimes the gifts we offer may be hidden and private, like cleaning the church, driving an elderly person to the store, visiting someone in the hospital, or bringing dinner to someone recently widowed.

Perhaps the primary place where the communal life of the Church is expressed is when we gather for worship. We gather on Sunday, the day of resurrection, to celebrate the Eucharist. This word, one we've heard often in our lives, means "to give thanks and praise." It reminds us that our primary purpose when we come together on Sunday is to give God our thanks and praise for the abundant graces and gifts of our lives. When we read the readings we are telling the story of God's faithfulness to us and to our ancestors. We are reminded that God continues to work in our lives and our world. Our hearts are moved with gratitude.

When we celebrate the Eucharist, it's not just us, this parish community, that offers our praise and thanks to God. We are also joined by the holy men and women of all times and ages as we unite ourselves with Christ, the Risen One, who lifts our prayer of praise to the Father. Throughout all time there is but one Eucharist, one Communion, that Christ offers to God. Every Mass we celebrate, every communion we receive, is part of that one, timeless Eucharist. Our voices are joined with those of our grandparents, great grandparents, all our loved ones, with those of Peter and Andrew, James, Matthew, Mother Teresa, and John XXIII when we gather around the altar on Sunday mornings.

THINGS TO CONSIDER

- Think about the men and women, living or dead, who've inspired you, encouraged you to live as a person of faith. Write down their names and how they've influenced your life.
- During the coming week you might pick up a copy of the Lives of the Saints and read some of their stories. Let their stories inspire you.
- Reflect on the personal gifts you bring to the Body of Christ.
- What can you contribute to the life of the community? How can you build up your parish family?

Take a few moments to write in your prayer journal.

CLOSING PRAYER

Imagine yourself standing before God surrounded by your loved ones and the holy ones of all the ages. Let yourself rest for awhile in humble reverence before the loving gaze of your Lord and God. This is the One who loves you much more than you know. All the ones around you are smiling. When you're ready, end with the following prayer, or better, with a prayer in your own words.

God of my heart,
you know me better than I know myself
and you understand that my heart
wants you to be more a part of my life.
Teach me, Lord,
as you would patiently teach a child,
how to allow you to permeate
my daily activities.
I don't think I yet comprehend
how much you love me
and want to have me close to you.
Thank you, Lord,
from the depths of my heart,
for those who journey beside me
as brothers and sisters.

Recognizing God's voice

SUGGESTED MUSIC

"Holy Darkness"

PREPARATION

Find a quiet place where you won't be disturbed. Most people find it easier to center and focus if they close their eyes and take deep, slow breaths. As you inhale, imagine that God is filling you with peace and joy. As you exhale, imagine that you are letting go of all anxiety and stress. Ask for the grace to learn how to be able to discern and recognize God's voice in your life.

When you're ready, continue by prayerfully reading the following reflection.

REFLECTION

Brothers and sisters: If you are led by the Spirit, you are not subject to the law....The fruit of the Spirit is love, joy, peace, patience, kindness, generosity, faithfulness, gentleness, and self-control. There is no law against such things....If we live by the Spirit, let us also be guided by the Spirit.

❧ GALATIANS 5:18–25

The challenge for anyone who desires to walk in God's presence is how to recognize the voice of God in the midst of all the other voices. This is important if we are sincere about our desire to follow God's gentle inspiration in our lives and to be companions of Jesus in his mission. We're speaking here, of course, about those subtle, quiet internal voices that each of us "feels" when we are attentive. What does God's voice feel like? How do we distinguish the voice of God from other voices? How do we know which inspiration comes from God and which comes from the Evil One?

Discerning God's voice in our lives requires attentiveness. The practice of the "examination of conscience," described in Contemplation Sixteen, is an effective way of paying attention to God's working in our daily lives. This is why this ritual was considered by Ignatius to be such an important spiritual practice for a person seeking union with God.

As we get to know someone, we become familiar with the ways they communicate, their tone of voice, their subtle non-verbal cues. More than anything, we begin to know their heart. The same is true in our relationship with God. As we spend time in prayer, we learn to recognize the inner voice of God. We can learn to discern God's voice by the way he communicates with us.

Discernment involves recognizing the interplay of consolation and desolation in our spiritual lives. If we make a list of the fruits of the spirit—charity, joy, peace, patience, kindness, goodness, faithfulness, gentleness—we'd have a good description of what "consolation" feels like. Ignatius defines consolation as every increase in faith, hope, and love, a feeling of interior joy that attracts us to God by filling us with peace and quiet joy. On the other hand, Ignatius defines desolation as entirely the opposite of consolation: darkness of soul, turmoil of spirit, an inclination to what is sinful and unhealthy, a feeling of restlessness that leads to a disturbance of our faith, a sense of hopelessness, and a lack of love.

Perhaps you'll notice that the words used here are feeling words. While we don't usually make decisions based on feelings, when we're talking of discernment, listening to our feelings is the key to recognizing God's voice in our lives. Feelings may be precarious to understand, but we must learn to discern them, because it is through feelings that we come to know how God speaks to us.

A practical example might help. Imagine that you're going through your day, perhaps even a difficult one, but you feel an inner peace. Then you get a phone call from a friend inviting you to be on a particular committee. Over the next few days, as you imagine yourself sitting at the committee meetings, you notice that you feel anxious, agitated, and gloomy. These feelings of "desolation" can be a pretty good indication that this is not where the Spirit of God is leading you.

Sometimes God will allow us to feel spiritual dryness, emptiness, barrenness so that we might experience our dependence on God. Even long periods of desolation in our prayer life can be God's way of emptying our souls of pride and arrogance so that we may recognize that consolation is God's gift and nothing we can earn or create on our own.

Ignatius encourages us to remember and hold on to times of great consolation when God seems so close and we feel that great inner joy and peace that comes from being with the One who loves us. The Enemy will always try to discourage us, to make us wonder if God has abandoned us, to tempt us to lose hope. If we remember those times of great consolation, we can draw comfort and hope from them even in the midst of our desolation.

THINGS TO CONSIDER

- Might I incorporate the practice of the examen into the routine of my day?
- Is there something I can do to make it a more natural part of my daily routine?
- Reflect on the interplay of consolation and desolation in your life. Are you presently experiencing consolation? Or are you feeling more desolation?

Make note of anything important in your prayer journal.

CLOSING PRAYER

Allow yourself to rest for a moment in the quiet, peaceful presence of the God who loves you more than you can imagine. This is the God who wants to be close to you and to share his heart with you. When you're ready, speak to God with the following prayer, or better, with your own words.

*G*reat and wonderful God,
I stand before you as your humble servant,
    wanting to hear your voice
and needing your help to guide my life.
Grant me the grace, Lord,
    to recognize when it is you who are
speaking in my life
and when it is the Evil Spirit
taunting and seducing me.
I want to follow your path of light and grace,
to be generous with my heart and my gifts,
and to bring the good news of your love
    to those who need it most.

Grace upon grace

SUGGESTED MUSIC
"As I Have Done for You"

PREPARATION

In crafting his *Spiritual Exercises*, St. Ignatius understood how important it is for a person not to move ahead without stopping occasionally to look back. In so doing, we draw spiritual nourishment from the consolation God has given us along the way. And so, rather than providing new material in this exercise, you are invited to read the notes you've made in your prayer journal to recall and savor those powerful moments of grace, allowing yourself to cherish them, and find even more goodness in them.

For some, this exercise might be a challenge and feel rather unsettling. Why waste time by going over what we've already done? We're so conditioned by our culture to keep moving ahead, always on to the next thing. In the life of the Spirit, however, remaining with any grace or consolation that's been given to us is never a waste of time. It's a way to nourish that deep-down hunger we prayed about in our very first exercise.

As always, prepare yourself by closing your eyes and breathing slowly and deeply for a few moments. As you feel yourself relax, take time to rest in the presence of the God who loves you. When you feel ready, move on to the reflection.

REFLECTION

Above all, maintain constant love for one another, for love covers a multitude of sins. Be hospitable to one another without complaining. Like good stewards of the manifold grace of God, serve one another with whatever gift each of you has received. Whoever speaks must do so as one speaking the very words of God; whoever serves must do so with the strength that God supplies, so that God may be glorified in all things through Jesus Christ. To him belong the glory and the power forever and ever. Amen.

❧ 1 PETER 4:8–11

Surrounded by the loving presence of God, look back at what you've written in your prayer journal for the previous nine exercises. Pay special attention to the notes you made at the very end of each exercise. This is where you tried to put into words the special goodness of that exercise, naming what you learned and how God drew your soul in prayer. As you read through your notes, make a list of the things that seem most significant to you.

For now, pick just one or two of them. Remember back to that moment and recall what it felt like. What was so significant about it? Why does it mean so much to you? Embrace it and savor it. Hold it in your heart with a quiet gratitude to God for gently teaching you and nurturing your soul. Don't feel compelled to rush forward. Even if you spend all the remaining time with these one or two graces, give yourself the opportunity to rest in God's infinite love and mercy. There's no need to figure anything out or draw a conclusion. Just be with God in the moment.

It's good to remind ourselves that whenever God gives us a consoling grace, it's not for us to hold and keep for ourselves. Graces are given to us to share—to bring light, peace, joy, and hope to others. The grace that we've been given is a grace that's meant to be given away so that it may become more grace for someone else.

If we read the account of the Last Supper in John's gospel, there's a very moving passage where Jesus is teaching us, his disciples, the most important things we need to remember when he is taken from our sight. This is his farewell address to us, his final instructions. He spells out for us the one most important thing: we should love each other as he has loved us. He doesn't just tell us to love each other, but to love as he himself has loved.

It's probably not a mistake that Jesus' farewell address is positioned in John's gospel immediately after the story about washing the disciples' feet. We might easily imagine Jesus saying to us, "If you want to understand what I mean by loving each other as I've loved you, remember what I just did. Do for each other what I have done." In other words, he teaches us that the way we show our love is by becoming servants of each other. Love shows itself in humble service, taking on those roles that no one else wants and being willing to get dirty knees.

THINGS TO CONSIDER

- What was the most significant grace of these last ten exercises?
- How can you hold onto the goodness of that and draw on its strength when the journey is difficult?
- Make a list, written in secret code, to put someplace you will see it this week, perhaps on your desk or taped to the refrigerator, to remind you all week of these wondrous graces of God.
- Take a moment to reflect on how you might share the grace of this spiritual journey with someone else, perhaps a spouse, a parent, a son or daughter, a co-worker.

Write your reflections in your prayer journal.

CLOSING PRAYER

Close your eyes and imagine Jesus' face before you. Imagine looking into his eyes and allowing him to look back into yours. As he looks into your heart, imagine him smiling with pride and delight in you. You are his beloved. End with the following prayer, or better, with a prayer in your own words.

*G*reat and generous Jesus, Lord of my life,
as I've looked back over the weeks
   of my journey with you
my heart is overwhelmed with gratitude.
Sometimes the steps you've taken with me
are so small that I hardly notice
   that we're moving forward.
But when I look back
I can see the distance we've come
   and how you've always been there
   at my side.
I pray that you help me be a good disciple,
using the consoling graces you've given me
to offer light, hope, and peace
to those who need it.

Faith that does justice

SUGGESTED MUSIC
"Blessed Are You"

PREPARATION

You are aware that prayer is more about learning to listen to what God has to say to us than it is about telling God what's on our minds. We are more able to listen when our souls are quiet and receptive. Spend a couple of minutes breathing deeply and centering your attention on God's loving presence. When you're ready to continue, prayerfully begin the following reflection.

REFLECTION

Jesus of Nazareth understood that not everyone would receive his message with an open mind and heart. In fact, there would be some who would, for one reason or another, directly criticize and oppose him. Even those in authority, hoping to find an error in his teaching, would publicly challenge him to defend what he preached. In the midst of such opposition, Jesus stood firm and stayed true to what God revealed in his heart.

Standing in the Jordan River at his baptism, Jesus heard the voice of God saying, "You are my beloved Son." This was his identity, and he tried to live and speak so as always to be true to this self-knowledge of who he was. When he saw in his heart that the Jewish scribes and Pharisees were teaching a kind of legalistic spirituality that was a burden to people, he felt compelled to speak against it. Even though he was steeped in the Jewish law and knew it well, he also knew that the law was only an expression of a person's relationship with God. Just because one kept every single prescription of the law, didn't necessarily mean that one's heart was true and holy.

Using the prayer of contemplation we've done in previous exercises, we want to be with Jesus in the following story. With our imagination, we'll enter the scene and experience it as if it were happening before our eyes. As we do this, we want to learn about Jesus and grow closer to him. Read the Scripture account slowly now, giving yourself the freedom to linger on any part that seems important. Let the story unfold in your imagination at your own pace. There's no need to rush.

> *Many of the Jews therefore, who had come with Mary and had seen what Jesus did, believed in him. But some of them went to the Pharisees and told them what he had done. So the chief priests and the Pharisees called a meeting of the council, and said, "What are we to do? This man is performing many signs. If we let him go on like this, everyone will believe in him, and the Romans will come and destroy both our holy place and our nation."*
>
> *But one of them, Caiaphas, who was high priest that year, said to them, "You know nothing at all! You do not understand that it is better for you to have one man die for the people than to have the whole nation destroyed."*
>
> *Jesus therefore no longer walked about openly among the Jews, but went from there to a town called Ephraim in the region near the wilderness; and he remained there with the disciples.*
>
> *Now the Passover of the Jews was near, and many went up from the country to Jerusalem before the Passover to purify themselves. They were looking for Jesus and were asking one another as they stood in the temple, "What do you think? Surely he will*

not come to the festival, will he?" Now the chief priests and the Pharisees had given orders that anyone who knew where Jesus was should let them know, so that they might arrest him.

When you've finished, deepen the meaning of the contemplation by prayerfully reading the following reflection.

Many of us would just as soon remain spiritually immature. It's much easier to let someone else in authority tell us what we should believe and how we should live our lives. By his example, Jesus calls us to a faith that is true to God's inner voice, what we sometimes call our conscience. As we spend time with Jesus, walking with him and watching him, our hearts become attuned to his. We learn to hear his voice leading us and guiding us. For many, this is a precarious way to live because there's always the possibility of being wrong. But it is the way that Jesus models for us.

Not many of us will be asked to match the heroism displayed by those who spilled their blood for Christ. These people courageously stood firm in their faith and stayed true to the inner voice of God. But we will occasionally be asked to stand as a witness to what we've come to know as true. Wherever there is injustice, poverty, hunger, enslavement, greed, or deception we'll be asked to stand up and speak out against it. There are times when it's right to confront and challenge what we know in our hearts to be wrong.

THINGS TO CONSIDER

- What did I find significant in this exercise? Was there anything that had special meaning for me?
- What did I learn about Jesus?
- Did I experience consolation or desolation during contemplation? Was I resistant at any point?
- Am I true to God's movement in my heart? Are there times when I want someone else to tell me what to do? Am I afraid of speaking up for fear of rejection?

Take a moment to write your reflections in your prayer journal.

Faith That Does Justice 87

CLOSING PRAYER

Close your eyes now and imagine yourself in the presence of Jesus. When you're ready, continue with the following prayer, or with a prayer in your own words.

Lord Jesus, my teacher and friend,
I so admire your courage and integrity
*   as you stay true to what God reveals*
in your heart,
even when it means facing opposition
and rejection, you stand firm in the truth
*   of God's love.*
Please, Lord,
teach me to have the same courage
and integrity.
Help me to trust God's voice
and to recognize it
amidst those opposing voices
*   that would try to convince me*
to believe something else.

God's word of hope

SUGGESTED MUSIC

"A Time Will Come for Singing"

PREPARATION

We begin our prayer time by centering ourselves in the presence of God. Find a quiet place where you won't be disturbed. Close your eyes for a few moments and breathe slowly as the Spirit of God surrounds you and fills you. If you find yourself distracted, irritated, or distressed, that's important because that's who you are at this moment. Pray for the grace to live in hope. When you're ready, prayerfully read the following reflection

REFLECTION

I consider that the sufferings of this present time are not worth comparing with the glory about to be revealed to us. For the creation waits with eager longing for the revealing of the children of God; for the creation was subjected to futility, not of its own will but by the will of the one who subjected it, in hope that the creation itself will be set free from its bondage to decay and will obtain the freedom of the glory of the children of God.

We know that the whole creation has been groaning in labor pains until now; and not only the creation, but we ourselves, who have the first fruits of the Spirit, groan inwardly as we wait for adoption, the redemption of our bodies.

For in hope we were saved. Now hope that is seen is not hope. For who hopes for what is seen? But if we hope for what we do not see, we wait for it with patience.

Imagine that overnight the life you know and love is wrenched from you by some terrible, unexpected tragedy. Events like this are devastating and certainly test our hope. Every one of us will have times when our hearts are brought to the brink of despair. The young psychiatrist Victor Frankl had a thriving practice in Vienna when the German army arrived and whisked him and thousands of others off to concentration camps. Every day there was a struggle simply to survive. The life he knew and loved was gone forever.

Frankl began to notice that many prisoners in the camp gave up very quickly, lost their will to live, and soon died. But there were others who quite surprisingly survived day after day with great hope and optimism. Curious about what enabled these survivors to keep going, the psychiatrist asked them about their state of mind and discovered that each and every one of them had something important to live for. One of them was in love and looked forward to the day he'd be reunited with his fiancée. Another prisoner had a retarded child and simply wanted to be alive to care for her. Frankl himself was working on a book when he was arrested and he wanted to live to be able to finish his work.

What is hope? We will all experience times in our lives when we are tempted to give up. When those times come, where will we find hope? When we are brought to our knees, what will we have to live for? It's important that we don't equate hope simply with a sunny optimism that things will turn out all right. Christian hope is so much more than that.

For the disciple of Jesus, hope stands side by side with despair. In fact, hope has no real meaning if at some point there isn't a real possibility of giving up. Hope has its most profound meaning when we are faced with difficulty, with tragedy, with death. Our hope is rooted in our understanding of the God whom Jesus revealed to us. It is based on fact, not fantasy.

Our God is one who has proved to be utterly reliable, always with us, never forsaking us. He is also a God of surprising wonders, the One for whom death will never be the final word. Even when all seems lost, God is there at our side with a love that promises to carry us through anything. In this sense, our hope is not arrogant, but truly humble, because it places our future in the hands of the God who loves us even to the end of time. We can look forward to great things from God because God has proven to be faithful in all things.

Hope is a great motivator because it is a vision of what might be possible. When we face great tragedies like the horrible, shocking disasters we experienced on September 11, 2001, our hearts fall in despair and we wonder if our world can ever survive such events. But our faith tells us that even in such times God has not left us and we can count on him to be there. God's promise sustains our hopeful expectation that out of the ashes of despair, God will help us rebuild our broken world, not just as it was before the tragedy, but even better, more peaceful, more just, and more loving than before.

THINGS TO CONSIDER

- What gives you hope? What is it that keeps you going? What do you live for?
- When have you faced the most difficult of times? How did God show himself to be faithful through these times?
- Do you live your days with hope? Do you offer hope to others? How do you contribute to the hope of your community of faith?

Spend a couple of moments writing your thoughts in your prayer journal.

CLOSING PRAYER

We'll now end this exercise by a more formal time of prayer where we speak directly to God, as a friend speaks to a friend. Pray to God using the words provided here, or better yet, in your own words.

God of hope and surprising wonders,
I stand here before you
clinging to your promise.
Sometimes my heart is so heavy
when I look at this dear world
that seems so broken.
All our efforts to repair it
seem so fruitless.
Please, Lord, be the anchor of my soul,
and teach me to labor patiently
at your side, as together we work
to recreate the face of the earth
and bring your kingdom to birth.

Faithful to our calling

SUGGESTED MUSIC
"Yahweh the Faithful One"

PREPARATION

Begin this exercise by finding a quiet place where you won't be disturbed. Close your eyes and take several long, slow deep breaths. Imagine that God's Spirit is entering your body and filling you with peace. If you find yourself distracted, it's okay. Sometimes distractions help us know what we should bring to God in prayer. They help us to be authentic before God and shouldn't be a cause for discouragement. Pray for the grace to be faithful to God's call to be a disciple of Jesus and faithful to the gifts he has given you. When you're ready, enter into the following reflection.

REFLECTION

> *I will sing of your steadfast love,*
> *O Lord, forever;*
> *with my mouth I will proclaim*
> *your faithfulness to all generations.*
> *I declare that your steadfast love*
> *is established forever;*
> *your faithfulness is as firm*
> *as the heavens.*
>
> PSALM 89:1–2

We live today in a consumer society that is dependent on many disposable items, things we use for awhile and then simply throw way. Infants today wear disposable diapers, rather than the kind we wash and reuse. When our cell phone is out of date, we buy a new, updated model. And when one of our socks gets a hole in it, we don't think about mending it, like our mothers once did. We just throw it away.

Luckily for us, God doesn't treat us as a disposable commodity. We are created in his image and are profoundly precious in his sight. God takes the time to repair our brokenness rather than throw us away. He will never discard us, even when we are old and infirm. God is faithful even when we are not.

Just as Jesus of Nazareth embodies for us the faithful love of our God, so we who are his disciples are summoned to this same faithfulness. We're called to live in such a way that we model the faithfulness of God to those entrusted to our care. Jesus doesn't discard people when they are no longer useful. And he doesn't abandon them when things get tough. God's faithfulness inspires us to be faithful. God's steadfast love calls forth our own.

We'll never know what it means to be bound by the gentle cords of covenant faithfulness unless we ourselves have responded to God's faithfulness to us. Like all virtues, we learn faithfulness through practice. And we really learn what faithfulness is when it is tested, when it would be easier for us to leave than to stay. The Old Testament is the story of the people of Israel testing God's covenant faithfulness in the face of rebellion, indifference, and unbelief. To say that God's faithfulness was tested by their rebellion, grumbling, and ingratitude would be an understatement.

Faithfulness and truth exist together and are profoundly related. Without truth, faithfulness is a sham. Faithfulness can thrive only where truth is told and where people are willing to live in the truth. True faithfulness exists when we are faithful even in the face of disappointment, mistrust, and deceit. Beyond this, faithfulness is the only context in which truth can be told. We find the courage to tell the whole truth when we know the other person is going to be there afterward, when we know they will not desert us if we reveal our truth.

It's very difficult to confront another person with the truth of their sin and betrayal. Yet at times our discipleship calls us to do this. We have very few opportunities to tell each other the truth of how our lives fall short of God's call to faith and justice, much less to encourage each other to greater love and service. But when the opportunity does arise, we should approach the other person with respect and humility, fully aware of our own shortcomings. Such an encounter can be a true opportunity to grow in our discipleship.

We learn faithfulness from those people in our lives who model it for us, especially our parents. Love is work. Unfortunately, some of us were not lucky enough to have good models of faithfulness. We learned that when relationships get difficult, it's time to hit the road. We have to work at our relationships, but that can't happen if we look for the door whenever it gets tough. The difficulties and challenges we experience are an opportunity for our love to grow deeper and truer. If we leave, that can never happen. People see in us how a disciple of Christ lives out his or her faith. Our faithfulness to our spouses, our families, our community, proves itself when it is tested, when we get angry or frustrated, when we're just plain tired.

THINGS TO CONSIDER

- Does the consumer attitude of our society enter into the way you relate to others? Do you sometimes use people only because they offer some value to you at the moment?
- Take a moment to make a list of all the people to whom you are bound by some kind of promise or commitment.
- Then make a second list of the people you feel you can rely on to be there for you no matter what.
- Compare the lists. What do they say about your life? What does your faithfulness mean to others? What does their faithfulness mean to you?

Spend a few moments writing your reflections in your journal.

CLOSING PRAYER

Now take some time to speak to God heart to heart, as a friend speaks to a friend. Use the prayer given here, or, better yet, pray in your own words.

*D*ear Lord, faithful friend and Savior,
I depend on your steadfast love and grace.
I would be lost without you.
I know, Lord, that I can always count on you,
especially in those times
when I feel lost and afraid.
Teach me, Jesus, how to be faithful
  as you are faithful,
  to love those you have given me
with steadfast care.
I want to be your faithful disciple.

The feast of heaven

SUGGESTED MUSIC
"Gather the People"

PREPARATION
Find a quiet place where you won't be disturbed. Begin by closing your eyes. Inhale slowly and deeply while imagining that God's presence is filling you. Then exhale slowly as you release any anxiety and tension. When you feel relaxed, pray for the grace to know Jesus more intimately, to understand his mind and heart, and to love him more deeply. When you're ready, continue with the reflection.

REFLECTION
Today we watch as Jesus and his friends gather to celebrate the Passover meal. As they sit around the table they're all aware of the growing controversy surrounding his teachings and have heard rumors that the Jewish authorities plan to silence him. Begin by reading through the gospel account once to recall it.

> *When the hour came, he took his place at the table, and the apostles with him. He said to them, "I have eagerly desired to eat this Passover with you before I suffer; for I tell you, I will not eat it until it is fulfilled in the kingdom of God." Then he took a cup, and after giving thanks he said, "Take this and*

divide it among yourselves; for I tell you that from now on I will not drink of the fruit of the vine until the kingdom of God comes." Then he took a loaf of bread, and when he had given thanks, he broke it and gave it to them, saying, "This is my body, which is given for you. Do this in remembrance of me." And he did the same with the cup after supper, saying, "This cup that is poured out for you is the new covenant in my blood. But see, the one who betrays me is with me, and his hand is on the table. For the Son of Man is going as it has been determined, but woe to that one by whom he is betrayed!" Then they began to ask one another which one of them it could be who would do this.

🔖 LUKE 22:14–23

Now close your eyes and use your imagination to enter into the story more deeply. Let the scene unfold in whatever way seems helpful for you. Don't be too concerned about staying strictly with the details of the story. The goal here is for you to see and experience what is happening, and making it real for yourself. Spend as much time as you want. There's no reason to rush even if you spend the entire time of prayer on this part.

When you're ready to move on, deepen the contemplation by prayerfully reading the following reflection.

Friends gather around a table to remember who they are and where they come from. These Jewish companions share a ritual meal, one they've celebrated many times before, and tell the story of the Passover, of how their ancestors escaped death by putting the blood of an unblemished lamb on their doorposts. Then Jesus takes some bread and a cup of wine and gives new meaning to this Passover meal.

In their document *Music in Catholic Worship*, the bishops of the United States have spoken of the importance of celebrating the Eucharist. "People in love make signs of love, not only to express their love but also to deepen it. Love never expressed dies. Christians' love for Christ and for one another and Christians' faith in Christ and in one another must be expressed in the signs and symbols of celebration or they will die" (Paragraph 4).

When we love someone, we go out of our way to remember their birthday, we keep in touch with phone calls or letters, we spend time with them, listen to their joys and sorrows, and we allow ourselves to grow in trust of their love. Little by little, we open our hearts to them, make ourselves vulnerable, and allow ourselves to be changed by their love. When we fail to do these things, our love fades and eventually dies.

In essence then, we go to Mass because we need to. It's what keeps our relationship with God alive and growing. At liturgy we express our love for God in signs and symbols. We sing songs that voice our praise. We tell stories that remind ourselves that we're the beloved ones of God. We share a meal of fellowship so that we might be nourished for our journey. We do all these things not just because they make us feel good but because they nurture our relationship with God.

As we contemplate the gospel account, we can imagine that Jesus would be thinking about these beloved friends he would soon leave behind. How he would miss them! And he wanted to reassure them that he was not leaving them alone. In an act of great love, he makes this ritual meal a means of communion with him. And so, any time we desire to be close to Jesus, we can gather around this eucharistic table and be united with him in his very flesh and blood.

THINGS TO CONSIDER

- What happened during your prayer? What was most important?
- What did you see and feel during the contemplation? What surprised you?
- Pause here to reflect on your experience of the Eucharist in your life of faith. How important a part does it play?
- Reflect for a moment how you participate in the Eucharist. Do you minister to the rest of the community? Or are you there just to receive?

CLOSING PRAYER

Finally, speak to God heart to heart, as a friend, using the following prayer, or, better yet, in your own words.

*D*earest Lord Jesus,
I am sometimes overwhelmed
by your desire to be close to us,
to be united with us in flesh and blood.
As we rehearse for the heavenly banquet
that we will one day share with you.
Help us to become each day
more and more the Body of Christ,
so that we embrace
in our communion with you
the reality of what we are.

God so loved the world

SUGGESTED MUSIC
"Behold the Wood"

PREPARATION
Find a quiet place where you won't be disturbed. As you close your eyes, concentrate on your breathing and imagine that you are taking in God's kindness and beauty as you breathe out all that is dark and stressful. Ask for the grace to be with Jesus as he suffers his passion and death. We want to carry in our hearts the image of Jesus doing all this for us. When you feel ready, continue with the reflection.

REFLECTION
First, read through the gospel account once to recall the details of the story.

> *Two others also, who were criminals, were led away to be put to death with him. When they came to the place that is called The Skull, they crucified Jesus there with the criminals, one on his right and one on his left. Then Jesus said, "Father, forgive them; for they do not know what they are doing." And they cast lots to divide his clothing. And the people stood by, watching; but the leader scoffed at him. The soldiers mocked him, coming up*

and offering him sour wine, and saying, "If you are the King of the Jews, save yourself!" There was also an inscription over him, "This is the King of the Jews."

One of the criminals who was hanged there kept deriding him and saying, "Are you not the Messiah? Save yourself and us!" But the other rebuked him, saying, "Do you not fear God, since you are under the same sentence of condemnation? And we indeed have been condemned justly, for we are getting what we deserve for our deeds, but this man has done nothing wrong." Then he said, "Jesus, remember me when you come into your kingdom." He replied, "Truly I tell you, today you will be with me in Paradise."

It was now about noon, and darkness came over the whole land until three in the afternoon, while the sun's light failed; and the curtain of the temple was torn in two. Then Jesus, crying with a loud voice, said, "Father, into your hands I commend my spirit." Having said this, he breathed his last.

🕊 LUKE 23:32–45

When you've finished, close your eyes and imagine yourself arriving on Calvary with the crowd. See the people, watch what they do, and listen to what they say. Allow yourself to become one of the characters in the story. The details are not as important as allowing yourself to experience it as if it's really happening to you. Stay with the story as long as you want. When you feel ready to move on, prayerfully read the following reflection.

It may be difficult for some of us to be with Jesus in his dying. Our culture tends to want to run from the reality of death, providing many ways for us to escape its finality. Even with all the death and violence that surrounds us, it makes us very uncomfortable. Very few of us have witnessed anyone's death or touched a cold, lifeless human body. This can make it more difficult for us to imagine ourselves looking up at Jesus hanging cold and lifeless on the cross.

Anytime death comes close to us we are reminded that death will come to all of us, to this world we know and love, to all the beauty, to everyone we love, and, finally, to our own body. All that we know and hold dear will one day die. While we may fear death and how it will come to visit us, the more difficult part is the profound loss and complete diminishment that we experience.

It's so hard for us to see Jesus, the one we've come to love so much, in such excruciating pain, lifting his body by his nailed wrists just to be able to take a few gasps of air into his lungs. It's almost too much to watch. If there was only something we could do, but there isn't. We find ourselves praying that God will end it all so that his pain will be over.

In all this, Jesus teaches us how to die. He shows us that, even in moments of great personal suffering, love has the power to reach beyond the pain to offer comfort, healing, forgiveness, and hope to others. Love is the only way to embrace death. Even in the awful loneliness, and the feelings of shame and devastating failure, Jesus doesn't respond with cynicism or resentment or anger. He embraces the suffering in his body as part of the human journey, our journey. He unites himself to all of us who will suffer and die. This is how much our God loves us.

THINGS TO CONSIDER
- What happened during your time of contemplation?
- What did you experience?
- What did you hear or see that you've never noticed before?
- Was this a time of consolation or desolation for you?

Take a few minutes to write in your prayer journal. Pause for a moment to reflect on how death is present in your experience. How has death touched you? What does it feel like? If you had a choice, how would you want to die? How do you want to face death? There may come a time when we're asked to be with someone as they die. How would you help them? What might you say or do? What have you learned about embracing death? Write your reflections here.

CLOSING PRAYER

As in previous exercises, we now end our time of reflection with a "colloquy," a heartfelt personal prayer to God. It should be like a friend talking to a friend. Begin with the words provided below, and then continue as your heart moves you.

Dearest Jesus, my Lord and friend,
  as I reflected on your suffering and death,
    I felt the deepest sorrow.
In your passion and death,
you showed the depth of your love,
I believe that you will be with me
as I face my own death
and the death of those I love.
Teach me, Lord, how to die.
Teach me how to embrace death
with love and grace.

Waiting with Mary

SUGGESTED MUSIC
"God My Savior"

PREPARATION
Following the pattern of past exercises, begin by finding a quiet place and spend a few moments centering yourself for this time of prayer. Close your eyes and take several slow, deep breaths. Imagine that you are breathing the Spirit of God into yourself. Ask God for the grace to trust God's promise. When you feel ready, continue with the reflection.

REFLECTION
In this exercise, using the same prayer of contemplation we've been learning, we'll place ourselves with Mary and the other disciples on Holy Saturday as they grieve the loss of their friend and Savior. There is no Scripture for us to follow, but we know that the friends of Jesus gathered in one place to grieve together.

Imagine a room with maybe fifteen people sleeping on the floor wherever there is space. The dim morning light is just beginning to filter though the windows. See what the room looks like and listen to the sounds of the early morning. There's still the sound of gentle snoring from one corner, but you notice that there's one person already awake, Peter, sitting with his back against the wall. You can tell that he's been awake for hours, maybe all night.

105

As the full morning sun fills the room, others begin to awaken. Slowly they open their eyes and sit up, eventually realizing where they are and remembering the horror of yesterday's events. They wish it had been a dream, but as they awaken they realize that what they fear is true: Jesus is dead. As they remember, their hearts break all over again.

As you look around you notice that over in one corner there's one very large pillow on which a beautiful middle-aged woman is reclining. You realize that it's Mary, the mother of Jesus. The others wanted her to have the one comfortable place to sleep because she's older and they can only imagine what she must be feeling. Her eyes too are red from weeping, but then you notice something else in her eyes. While there's sadness, there's also a look of peace and quiet faith. It's the look of someone who trusts that somehow this is all part of God's mystery and that God will find a way to bring good from all this pain.

Some of the women have brought food and begin preparing something to eat. The smells begin to fill the room. No one is speaking much, but a few of the disciples are quietly conversing. You can't really hear what's being said, but from the look on their faces you know what's in their hearts. They're wondering what to do now that he's gone. Where do they go? Do they stay together? What would he want them to do? Some are feeling so ashamed for having deserted him when the soldiers came to arrest him in the garden. Several of the twelve are not even here out of fear or guilt. And there's the question of whether the authorities will now come looking for them, too.

We look over at Mary again, with the disciple John sitting close by. He has not left her side for even a moment since they arrested Jesus. Others are coming up to speak with her, possibly to offer their condolences and share their grief, but surely to be fed by her faith. She has never doubted God's love. Here's a woman who was visited by an angel who told her she would bear a son even though she was a virgin. She watched in wonder when shepherds and visitors from far away came to worship her newborn infant in the stable cave. She fled with Joseph to Egypt when an angel told him that they must go there to save the baby's life. In all these moments she placed herself in God's hands and trusted completely that God's love would accomplish what was right.

But her son, her Messiah too, was now dead. She had held his lifeless body in her lap when they took him from the cross. They had laid him in that cold, dark tomb and closed the entrance. How could this be part of God's plan? As she prayed for faith, she remembered the song she sang after the angel came to visit her as a young woman. She found herself singing it again in the quiet of her heart and it brought her peace. "My soul proclaims the greatness of the Lord."

Stay with the contemplation for as long as it seems fruitful. Just let the scene unfold for you and allow it to fill your heart. Even if you just sit in silence watching and waiting with the others, that's fine. Silent waiting is the best way to pray on Holy Saturday. When it feels right, continue reading the reflection.

THINGS TO CONSIDER

- What was most significant in this contemplation? What was it that most moved your heart and your imagination?
- Did you experience consolation? Desolation? Were you distracted?
- What can you carry with you that will help you live your life with more trust in God's promise to always bring life from death?

Spend a few minutes writing what seemed important to you in your prayer journal.

CLOSING PRAYER

As in previous exercises, we now end our time of reflection with a "colloquy," a heartfelt prayer in the presence of God. It should be like a friend talking to a friend. Begin with the words provided below, and then continue as your heart may move you.

*D*earest Lord Jesus,
   it breaks my heart
   to watch your friends today.
   They were so devastated by your death
   and felt so completely lost.
   They didn't know what to do with their grief,
   but your mother is amazing in her faith.
   I don't understand
   how she could be so strong.
   It seems that nothing could shake her faith,
   or her great trust
   that God's love will always prevail.
   Lord, teach me to have that kind of faith.
   Teach me to surrender my life into your hands.

Daring to dance

SUGGESTED MUSIC
"Join in the Dance"

PREPARATION
Begin this exercise by finding a quiet place where you won't be disturbed. Close your eyes as you take some long, slow deep breaths. Imagine yourself breathing the peace of God's Spirit into your soul. Then ask for the grace to experience the joy and wonder of the resurrection of Jesus. When you're ready, continue with the following reflection.

REFLECTION
Read the gospel account once, recalling the details of the story.

When the Sabbath was over, Mary Magdalene, and Mary the mother of James, and Salome bought spices, so that they might go and anoint him. And very early on the first day of the week, when the sun had risen, they went to the tomb. They had been saying to one another, "Who will roll away the stone for us from the entrance to the tomb?" When they looked up, they saw that the stone, which was very large, had already been rolled back. As they entered the tomb, they saw a young man, dressed in a white robe, sitting on the right side; and they were alarmed.

🖉 MARK 16:1–5

But the angel said to the women, "Do not be afraid; I know that you are looking for Jesus who was crucified. He is not here; for he has been raised, as he said. Come, see the place where he lay. Then go quickly and tell his disciples, 'He has been raised from the dead, and indeed he is going ahead of you to Galilee; there you will see him.' This is my message for you." So they left the tomb quickly with fear and great joy, and ran to tell his disciples.

         🖋 MATTHEW 28:5–8

Now close your eyes and experience the story with your imagination. The sun is just beginning to show itself on the horizon. Follow the women as they make their way to the tomb. Let the scene unfold before you. Become one of the characters in the story and let the event enter your heart. Even if you spend the whole time of prayer on this part, move forward only when you're ready.

As the sun rises, the women leave to carry out the ritual embalming. They had prepared themselves for this heartbreaking yet loving task, knowing that they would soon be touching the cold, lifeless body of their Lord. They make their way in silence, preparing themselves for the sacred ritual they are about to perform.

And yet, sometimes God turns our world upside down and shatters our expectations. They aren't prepared for what they see next. As the women round the bend and have first sight of the tomb, they see the stone has been moved from the entrance. How strange! Who moved it? And where are the Roman soldiers ordered to guard the entrance?

They hurry inside the cave to find a young man standing there in shining white robes. They're startled and afraid. As the man speaks, their minds and hearts struggle to comprehend his words. "Jesus… the crucified one…he's not here…raised from death…he'll meet you in Galilee…tell the disciples." His voice is kind, almost trembling, as if he's well aware of the profound message he's delivering to the world. He keeps reassuring them to not be afraid.

Their hearts are already tender from days of grieving. Now they're being told something that seems so utterly impossible. All at once they want to cry out with uncontrolled joy, but then they hesitate. It just doesn't make sense. They want so badly to believe that it's true. They have no time to think this through. Their minds are racing and their hearts are pounding, as they run back to tell the others.

The Enemy thought he had won. The Beloved of God was dead. But the victory of death was not to be savored for very long because there is one power that even death cannot silence. Of course, the Enemy knows nothing of this power because it's foreign to him. It's the power of love. At the moment of Jesus' final breath, the great and mighty God, the Lord of all creation, bowed his head and wept. His beloved one, his son, had died a human death and was no more. But love could not let this be the end of the story.

Because God's love is stronger than death, death will never be the final word. All that is human and good and beautiful in us will be raised up from the tomb of death because we're not created for death. We were created out of love, created for love, and find our final destiny in a love that is eternal. Along with Jesus, we are all the beloved of God and will share the victory of Jesus over death. That is the heart of God.

God's victory over sin and death is not yet complete, and so we must hold fast to our faith in Jesus' victory. We cannot escape death, for it is our destiny, and that of all creation, to journey through death and rise with Jesus from the cold, dark tomb to live forever in the love of God.

THINGS TO CONSIDER

- What did I experience during this time of contemplation? Was this a time of consolation or desolation for me?
- Have I ever had something happen that was hard to understand, something extraordinary and profound, something that really affected me deeply?
- Do I live my life with an Easter faith?

Take a few minutes to write in your prayer journal.

CLOSING PRAYER

As in previous exercises, we now end our time of reflection with a "colloquy," a heartfelt prayer in our own words. Begin with the words suggested below, and then continue as your heart moves you.

Dearest Lord Jesus,
my heart so wants to know
the joy of Easter,
to share the excitement
of your first disciples
as they heard the message of the angel.
I know I will struggle at times in my faith
when life is difficult
and hope is hard to find.
But I know and believe deep in my heart
that God's love will never allow
any of us to remain forever
in the tomb of death.

Feed my sheep

SUGGESTED MUSIC
"Here I Am, Lord"

PREPARATION
Begin by closing your eyes and breathing deeply for a few moments as a way of centering yourself. When your soul feels quiet, ask for the grace to experience a deepening joy that Jesus, our friend and savior, is alive and risen. We want to be aware of his presence as we take this good news to the world. When you're ready, continue with the reflection.

REFLECTION
We'll again use the kind of imaginative prayer we've learned from Ignatius to enter into this story from the gospel. Read through the passage once to recall the words and events. Then close your eyes and allow the scene to come alive in your imagination. Do not feel any need to hurry, or to stay with the details of the story. God's Spirit will lead you where you most need to go. Stay with the contemplation as long as it seems good, even if it takes the entire time of prayer.

> *Gathered there together were Simon Peter, Thomas called the Twin, Nathanael of Cana in Galilee, the sons of Zebedee, and two others of his disciples. Simon Peter said to them, "I am going*

*fishing." They said to him, "We will go with you." They went out
and got into the boat, but that night they caught nothing.*

*Just after daybreak, Jesus stood on the beach; but the disciples
did not know that it was Jesus. Jesus said to them, "Children,
you have no fish, have you?" They answered him, "No." He said
to them, "Cast the net to the right side of the boat, and you will
find some." So they cast it, and now they were not able to haul
it in because there were so many fish. That disciple whom Jesus
loved said to Peter, "It is the Lord!" When Simon Peter heard
that it was the Lord, he put on some clothes, for he was naked,
and jumped into the lake. But the other disciples came in the
boat, dragging the net full of fish....*

*When they had gone ashore, they saw a charcoal fire there,
with fish on it, and bread. Jesus said to them, "Bring some of
the fish that you have just caught." So Simon Peter went aboard
and hauled the net ashore, full of large fish, a hundred and
fifty-three of them; and though there were so many, the net was
not torn. Jesus said to them, "Come and have breakfast." Now
none of the disciples dared to ask him, "Who are you?" because
they knew it was the Lord. Jesus came and took the bread and
gave it to them, and did the same with the fish. This was now
the third time that Jesus appeared to the disciples after he was
raised from the dead.*

$\bullet$ JOHN 21:2–14)

After the extraordinary events that occurred in Jerusalem over
Passover, the disciples of Jesus returned home to Galilee. Surely
they were still trying to absorb the meaning of everything they had
seen. And so, while they figured out what to do next, they decided
to do what they knew best, what was familiar. Peter leads the way
for the others and says that he's going fishing. The others tag along.
And it's while they're doing what is familiar that they meet the Ris-
en Jesus.

Like the disciples, we don't always know what to do next in our
lives. Often we don't need to do anything extraordinary or even

anything new, to experience the presence of the Risen Lord. He comes to meet us right in the midst of our normal activities and works wondrous miracles for us right where we are. He sits with us to share a meal of friendship.

Though these experienced fishermen had caught nothing all night, they trusted his voice. And because they responded, taking a risk to do something that seemed useless, they brought in a catch that was beyond their expectations. And then they knew it was he. They had learned to recognize him in the wonders he worked in their lives. So he is with us, as we have learned to recognize him, because we've walked with him through these spiritual exercises.

All during breakfast on the beach, Peter had avoided looking at Jesus, but he knew Jesus was watching him. The shame of his denial in the courtyard outside Herod's palace gnawed at his soul. As always, Jesus understood him so well. "Simon, do you love me?" asks Jesus. "Lord, you know that I love you." Jesus knew that Peter needed to hear himself say this and asked him to do it twice more. The Risen Lord doesn't chastise Peter for his fearful betrayal, but simply needs to hear Peter say the words, "I love you." And then, Jesus sends Peter and the rest on their mission of discipleship, "Feed my sheep."

THINGS TO CONSIDER

- What was your experience of this contemplation? What seemed significant for you?
- Was it a time of consolation or desolation?
- Have you learned to recognize the presence of the Risen Lord in your life?
- Where and when have you seen him working wonders?

Spend a couple of minutes writing in your prayer journal.

CLOSING PRAYER

Stand in humble reverence before the loving gaze of the Risen Jesus. This is the Lord who loves you so much more than you know. He does not chastise you for your failures, but simply needs to hear your words of love. End with the following prayer, or better, with a prayer in your own words.

Risen Lord and Savior,
  I'm still trembling with joy
  to know that you are alive and risen.
  I'm afraid that I'll wake up
  and find this is all a dream.
  Even though my faith is sometimes weak,
    and I get afraid
  when others laugh at my hope,
    I know you'll work wonders in my life
    when I respond to your invitation.
  Lord, know that I love you,
    and will do my best
    to feed your little ones.

Living in the Spirit

SUGGESTED MUSIC
"Send Us Your Spirit"

PREPARATION
Find a quiet place where you won't be disturbed. Most people find it easier to focus if they close their eyes. Take slow, deep breaths, imagining as you inhale that God is filling you with peace and joy. Likewise, as you exhale imagine that you are letting go of all your anxiety and stress. Continue for a couple of minutes. Then ask for the grace to become aware of the presence of the Spirit of the Risen Lord in your life. When you're ready, continue with the following reflection.

REFLECTION
After the resurrection, the disciples of Jesus had to learn a new relationship with him. They were used to experiencing a flesh and blood human being whom they could see and touch. But now things had changed. His body was different. Though they could still see and hear and touch him, he could appear and disappear from their midst. He had told them that he would be leaving but would give them his Holy Spirit.

In the Hebrew Testament, the word for "spirit" is *ruach*. A Jewish person hearing this word would understand it to mean something close to our word "breath," a moving wind that carries the life of a being. It isn't a static concept, but rather a dynamic one. When Jesus says that He will send his "Holy Spirit" to the disciples, he is essentially saying that he will give them his own "living breath" to be their comfort and their companion.

In one of the previous exercises we prayed to be attentive to God's gentle inspiration for us. We're speaking here, of course, about those subtle, quiet internal voices that each of us feels when we are attentive. These are the movements of God's Spirit and sometimes the spirit of the Evil One in our lives. If we're sincere about following God's way for us, the challenge is how to recognize God's Spirit as it lives and breathes and moves in our lives.

The best way to recognize the presence of the Holy Spirit is by the way in which the Spirit manifests itself in people's lives. Paul calls these the "fruits" of the Spirit and names the important ones in his letter to the Galatians—love, joy, peace, patience, kindness, goodness, faithfulness, gentleness, and self-control. When these qualities are present, we know that God's Spirit is there. Likewise, we can be sure that God doesn't inspire indifference, gloominess, turmoil, intolerance, meanness, wickedness, unfaithfulness, violence, and self-indulgence.

The breath of God can also enable us to step outside ourselves, giving us great power and wisdom to do things that are far beyond our innate abilities.

When the day of Pentecost had come, they were all together in one place. And suddenly from heaven there came a sound like the rush of a violent wind, and it filled the entire house where they were sitting. Divided tongues, as of fire, appeared among them, and a tongue rested on each of them. All of them were filled with the Holy Spirit and began to speak in other languages, as the Spirit gave them ability.

Now there were devout Jews from every nation under heaven living in Jerusalem. And at this sound the crowd gathered and was bewildered, because each one heard them speaking in the native language of each. Amazed and astonished, they asked,

"Are not all these who are speaking Galileans? And how is it that we hear, each of us, in our own native language?"

Awe came upon everyone, because many wonders and signs were being done by the apostles.

✹ ACTS 2:1–8, 43

The effect of God's Holy Spirit on these disciples was truly profound. Just a few moments earlier, these friends of Jesus were huddling in fear and confusion, wondering how they would carry out the mission given them by Christ. And suddenly they become passionate, influential messengers of the good news of the resurrection. The Breath of God transforms them, giving their words a power far beyond what the disciples themselves were ever capable of.

In the account of Pentecost, it says that the Spirit came upon the disciples "like the rush of a violent wind." In other words, it was an experience that startled them out of their security and shook them up in a way they couldn't have imagined. Sometimes we too can become settled into a kind of safe, uneventful kind of Christianity. Sometimes our hearts become hardened with the ache of the world. And then the Spirit urges us, sometimes quietly, sometimes forcefully, to step out of our familiar world.

THINGS TO CONSIDER

Take the time to go back and review Exercise 19, where we reflected on what Ignatius calls the "discernment of spirits." It was the first step in learning to recognize the movement of God's Spirit in our lives.

- Have I noticed the Spirit working in my life? Have there been times when I know there's a power more than me at work?
- How might I pay more attention to the working of God's spirit in my life? Do I allow God's spirit to influence the way I make decisions?

Take a few moments to write in your prayer journal.

CLOSING PRAYER

Allow yourself to rest for a moment in the quiet, peaceful presence of God. Listen to the Spirit of Life enter your very soul with every breath. When you're ready, speak to God with the following prayer, or better, with your own words.

Great and loving God,
   sometimes we just aren't prepared
   when you send your "mighty wind"
into our lives.
Lord, I want to pay attention
to your Holy Breath
   as it leads me and inspires me
   to live courageously as a disciple of Jesus.
With my meager gifts and timid heart,
   I don't always feel up to that mission, Lord.
But I know that your Spirit will fill me
   and make up for what I lack.
Teach me, Lord, to recognize your voice
and to follow your quiet,
and sometimes powerful, promptings.
Help me to move beyond my fear.

The path before us

SUGGESTED MUSIC

"These Alone Are Enough"

PREPARATION

Prepare yourself by finding a quiet place, closing your eyes, and imagining yourself in the holy presence of the God who created you and has loved you at every moment. If you just want to sit silently in God's presence for awhile, allow yourself to do that. Ask for the grace to have a deep awareness of all the ways that God has loved you throughout your life. When you're ready to move forward, prayerfully continue with the reflection.

REFLECTION

In this final exercise we'll once more follow the example of Ignatius of Loyola who, at the end of his *Spiritual Exercises*, invites us into a contemplation of God's love. To do this you'll reflect on all the places you've been since you began this journey with Jesus. In the remembering you'll become aware of how God has drawn you into more intimacy and this will provide an opportunity to treasure the graces that God has given you.

Open the prayer journal you've kept during the previous twenty-nine exercises. This is where you tried to put into words the special goodness of each prayer exercise for you, to name what you learned and how God drew your soul into prayer. In the presence of God, read through what you've written, remembering the times of grace and savoring them again. Tell God how grateful you are for what you've experienced. Spend as much time with this as seems fruitful. If it takes the whole time of prayer, that's fine.

Many people, when they'd come to the end of Spiritual Exercises, would write Ignatius and ask his advice as they faced the challenge of continuing to find intimacy with God in the midst of their busy daily activities. Ignatius would tell them that the answer was to become a "contemplative in action." By this he meant that the two realms, intimacy in prayer and our daily activities, don't need to be separate parts of our lives. He encouraged them to find God in all things, to connect with God right in the midst of their daily activities, not just during formal times of prayer. In doing this, a person learns that one can pray all through the day.

Ad majorem Dei gloriam ("for the greater glory of God") is the motto of St. Ignatius. For him, the response to God's unconditional, unfailing love is to do not just the minimum, but rather to do what is greater, what is more, the *magis*, as Ignatius calls it. Since God has loved us so much, we want to place ourselves at his service, to do whatever we do for God's greater glory. In Ignatius' mind, there are often many good things that we might do as disciples. But for him the choice is always to do what will accomplish the greater good and be for God's greater glory.

Ignatius would have a person consider three questions as a way of focusing our living out our response to God's faithful love:

- What have I done for Christ?
- What am I doing for Christ?
- What more ought I do for Christ?

Take a moment of quiet at this point to consider these three questions for yourself. This is not an inventory of our discipleship, but rather a heartfelt response to God's goodness and grace. As we've come to know and love Jesus, we can be more and more generous with our response to him.

These exercises have been a journey of growing in intimacy and friendship with Jesus. We've done the work of placing ourselves with Jesus as his companions, and we've followed, watched, and listened to him as he goes about his ministry. We've learned much about his heart and we've grown to love him more and more. When we fall in love with someone, we grow to trust that person with our heart, with our future, with our very life. We allow ourselves to become vulnerable and surrender what is most precious to us into the hands of the other. In other words, we give ourselves away.

And so St. Ignatius, at the very end of his *Spiritual Exercises*, has us pray a powerful prayer of self-surrender as we offer ourselves to God. The only thing that makes such an offering possible is knowing—not just in our mind but in the very depth of our heart—how much God loves us. Without a knowledge of that infinite love, we would be too afraid, too distrustful, to even think of surrendering ourselves in such a profound way. And so, with Ignatius' prayer of offering, we give back to the infinite God all that we are and all that we have.

THINGS TO CONSIDER

- How can I form the habit of being mindful of God in the midst of my daily activities and becoming a contemplative in action?
- What habits have I formed in doing these exercises that can help me accomplish this?
- What are some things I can use to remind me of God during the day?
- How can I begin and end my day with God, or even learn how to have brief thirty-second conversations with God during the day?

Spend a few minutes writing your reflections in your prayer journal.

CLOSING PRAYER

Close your eyes and imagine yourself in the presence of the eternal God. Imagine looking into his eyes and allowing him to look back into yours. As he looks into your heart, imagine him smiling with pride and delight in you. You are his beloved. Then pray Ignatius'

Suscipe, the prayer where we surrender our lives and all we hold into God's hands.

Take, Lord, and receive all my liberty,
my memory, my understanding,
and my entire will,
all that I have and possess.
You have given all to me.
To You, Lord, I return it.
Everything is yours;
dispose of it according to your will.
Give me only your love and your grace.
That is enough for me.

Listed below are albums by Dan Schutte that contain the songs listed in this book

PRINCE OF PEACE
Beyond the Moon and Stars
Christ Circle Round Us
Come, O Lord
Come, Lord Jesus
God My Savior
Prince of Peace
A Time Will Come for Singing

ALWAYS AND EVERYWHERE
See the Lilies
You Are Near

GLORY IN THE CROSS
As I Have Done for You
Blessed Are You
Dayenu Litany
Litany of Saints
We Will Journey in Faith

MORNING LIGHT
Gather the People
Give Us Faith, Lord
These Alone Are Enough

LORD OF LIGHT
Here I Am, Lord
Only This I Want

GOD'S HOLY GIFTS
Come with Me into the Fields

HERE I AM, LORD ANTHOLOGY
Behold the Wood
Here I Am, Lord
Only This I Want
Send Us Your Spirit
Yahweh, the Faithful One
You Are Near

LOVER OF US ALL
God of Love
Holy Darkness
So the Love of God

TABLE OF PLENTY ANTHOLOGY
Beyond the Moon and Stars
Christ Circle Round Us
For the Beauty
Holy Darkness
Join in the Dance

DRAWN BY A DREAM
For the Beauty
Join in the Dance
Pilgrim Companions

THE STEADFAST LOVE
I Found the Treasure
Send Us Your Spirit

GENTLE NIGHT
A Time Will Come for Singing

AVAILABLE FROM | **OCP** *(1-800-548-8748, www.ocp.org)*
Pilgrim Music *(91-866-851-5391, www.pilgrimmusic.com)*